THE PATH OF
Intercession

PHILIP BROWN

THE PATH OF
Intercession

PHILIP BROWN

Table of Contents

Foreword 1

Dedication 5

The Power of God's Spirit 7

Good News.. 11

Chapter 1: Living in Union with God –
The Foundation of All Intercession.................................... 13

Chapter 2: Authority in Intercession –
Praying from Your Position in Christ 19

Chapter 3: The Practice of the Presence of God –
A Life of Unceasing Prayer... 25

Chapter 4: Partnering with the Holy Spirit –
The Intercessor's Guide to Supernatural Prayer 31

Chapter 5: The Healing Power of God – Manifesting
Today through Intercession 37

Chapter 6: Pressing Through – The Power
of Persistence in Intercession... 45

Chapter 7: Thanksgiving, Praise, and Worship –
Unlocking Heaven's Power in Intercession....................... 51

Chapter 8: Prophetic Intercession –
Declaring God's Will with Authority................................. 57

Chapter 9: Bringing change through Intercession 63

Chapter 10: Fasting and Intercession—Accelerating...................... 67

Chapter 11: The Rewards of Perseverance
in Intercession... 73

Chapter 12: Leaving a Legacy of Intercession 79

Chapter 13: Walking in the Full Authority
of Your Calling as an Intercessor 85

Chapter 14: The Power of a Pure Heart – Building
Strong Character in the Life of an Intercessor 89

Chapter 15: William Branham – The Prophetic and Healing
Power of God in Action.. 97

Chapter 16: John Wesley – Revival through
Prayer and Holiness.. 103

Chapter 17: Billy Graham – A Voice for
Evangelism and Global Revival 109

Chapter 18: John G. Lake – A Life of Faith,
Healing, and Intercession.. 117

Chapter 19: Smith Wigglesworth – The Minister
of Faith and Miracles.. 125

Chapter 20: John Alexander Dowie – The Path
to Divine Healing.. 131

Chapter 21: Jesus, the Ultimate Intercessor –
Miracles Born from Prayer... 139

Chapter 22: Paul the Apostle – An Intercessor Empowered by
Signs, Wonders, and Miracles 147

Chapter 23: Intercession in the Heart of Darkness –
Praying in Hitler's Office 155

Chapter 24: The Book of Hebrews –
The Call to Deeper Things... 163

Chapter 25: John, the Apostle of Love –
Running with Jesus to the End 169

Chapter 26: The Tabernacle of Moses and the Holy of Holies.................. 179

Chapter 27: The Throne Room of God – The Intersection
of Power, Presence, and Purpose 185

About the Author.. 197

FOREWORD

It is with profound joy and the utmost admiration that I write this foreword for my dear friend, Philip Brown. Over the past decade, I have witnessed firsthand his strong devotion to the Lord and have been consistently moved by his steadfast hope and integrity. Philip's life testifies to the transformative power of God's grace—a grace he not only believes in but actively demonstrates through his passionate commitment to intercession.

Philip's perspective on intercessory prayer is both insightful and convicting, and it is this very passion that drives the pages of this book. The Path of Intercession is not merely a work of theology; it speaks a deep truth and provides a profound yet accessible guide to those seeking to cultivate a life of prayer with purpose. It meticulously examines the crucial distinction between an intercessor and the act of intercession itself.

I am confident it will become a vital resource for those longing to deepen their understanding of prayer. Within these pages, Philip's practical insights illuminate how to transition from being spiritually curious to powerful, Spirit-filled intercession.

I recommend this work to people everywhere, particularly those who sense a divine prompting to enter a deeper spiritual walk. May this book strengthen your resolve, equip you with spiritual authority, and increase your boldness in prayer—knowing that your intercession has the extraordinary power to change the world around you and influence the course of history.

Abi Abibula
Teacher, Leader, and Minister from Trinidad and Tobago

It is my honour to write this foreword for *The Path of Intercession*, a book that resonates deeply with anyone longing to see the transforming power of God in their life and the world around them.

It's wonderful to have a friend and brother in Christ like Philip Brown. Phil has been such a blessing to me, and it's my prayer that God would gift everyone with a friend like him. I first met Phil back in our school of ministry days. We both lived on one of the roughest streets in Redding, California. It was the perfect place to see God move. Phil and I took that to heart. God gave me the pleasure and honour of walking with Phil during those times. His passion and love for Jesus is infectious. We spent many moments together as students talking and sharing about Jesus with each other. Many times, we would end up sharing testimonies of God's miraculous power. If we ever needed more encouragement, we would share testimonies of past moves and people of God. Jesus was never far from our conversation.

That was over 10 years ago. In recent times, I've stayed connected with Phil. Like me, he has gone through a process of maturity and refinement. We have both gone through hardship and difficulty, to say the least. However, together we have been able to talk and encourage each other in the midst of our difficulty. Like old times, Jesus has not been far from our conversation.

What encourages me most about Phil is that he continues pursuing God. He still has a passion for Jesus, he values the Word of God, his character and integrity have been untainted by the hardships and difficulties of this world. Most of all, he still loves Jesus and believes in the power of the gospel! I, like Phil, have seen many miracles of God. I have seen God heal cancer, dissolve metal in people's bodies, and even heal terminal illness. However, I also consider it to be a miracle when someone goes through great hardship but still possesses a love for Christ and His gospel. I love to hear about those kinds of testimonies too! I cannot deny that Phil's life demonstrates a testimony of God.

It's easy to lose hope and faith when you look at the hardships and darkness of this world; not so easy when you fix your eyes on Jesus. That is why this book brings to light the importance of intercession. There are so many situations in our world that need a touch from Jesus right now. While reading Phil's book, my convictions were powerfully stirred up. I believe Christ wants to transform this world. *The Path of Intercession* helped to reignite my faith for such things. The insights, revelations, and testimonies found in this book will encourage you to seek Christ.

I have read many articles and books on prayer and intercession. They often leave me with nice thoughts and empty theories without any real plan to put them into practice. One of the most striking aspects of this book is its ability to balance profound theological truths with practical steps for stepping into intercession. Phil's book takes to heart the truth found in 1 Corinthians 4:20: "The Kingdom of God is not a matter of talk, but of power." While reading this book, I began to experience the renewing and equipping power of Christ to change the world.

I think people reading this book will experience the infectious passion that Phil has for the truth, the power of God, and for Jesus. Reading this book felt just like my school of ministry days when Phil talked about the testimonies of God and shared Jesus with me. Phil would often leave me with a hunger to see God move in my life after I talked with him. It was a burning hunger that came from the Holy Spirit. May you know that same burning hunger after reading this book.

It's my prayer that as you read this book, you will be deeply impacted by God. After reading this book, may you be equipped to intercede for our world. May you step into everything that God has made you to be. May God bless you with a filling of His Spirit as you read this book. May you know the words of God as you grasp the calling to which God is leading you. May you always know Christ and know Him crucified.

With blessings,

Lee Woodward

(Speaker, teacher, pastor, and leader from the UK)

DEDICATION

To my friends at **Metro Church of Kansas City**,
you will always be family to me.

To the many **Fathers, Mothers, and mentors** who
have shaped my life—especially **Teresa Butrous** and **Bob
and Debby Spruill**—your guidance and encouragement
have helped form the foundation of my faith and certainly
changed the course of my life. What you do has a bigger
impact than you will ever fully know.

To my **parents**, whose hard work and sacrifice is incredible.
Your love and perseverance have shaped my journey.

To my **grandfather, Marvin Brown**, and my **Great Uncle,
Charles N. Sharpe**, two men who inspired me profoundly as role models.
Your unique and inspirational qualities continue to guide and inspire me.

Most of all, to my sons, **Judah and Ian**. Being your dad is God's greatest
gift to me. You are both incredible men, and I am so blessed to have
you. This book is dedicated to you, with love, pride, and the hope that
you will always know the depth of God's love and purpose for your lives.

THE POWER OF GOD'S SPIRIT

When we talk about the power to change the world around us, many people think of influence through wealth, politics, or social status. But there's a deeper, more profound kind of power that anyone can experience—a power that doesn't just impact one's inner life, but can also have a real, tangible effect on the world around them. It's a power that can heal, transform, and change circumstances that seem impossible.

You see, when an individual is fully connected to something greater than themselves—when they're living in harmony with a divine source of strength and love—there's an undeniable shift that happens. This isn't just a matter of personal development or self-help. It's about a real power that flows through a person's life and starts to impact everything they touch. It can be felt in their words, their actions, and even in the atmosphere around them. People begin to notice that something is different, that there's an authority and grace in their life that can't be explained by human effort alone.

This power has the ability to bring peace in the middle of chaos. It can restore what's broken—whether that's a person's health, a relationship, or even a situation that seems completely hopeless. It's the kind of power that can transform despair into hope, sickness into health, and weakness into strength. And it's not confined to one individual. When someone is truly filled with this power, it overflows into the lives of those around them.

Think about it this way: Just as a light bulb radiates light to the surrounding space, someone who is connected to this divine source radiates a different kind of energy—one that can influence hearts, heal wounds, and bring clarity where there was confusion. It's as though the atmosphere changes when they walk into a room. There's a peace that settles, or a sense of expectation that rises. You've probably felt it before—being in the presence of someone who seems to carry something beyond themselves.

This power is not about domination or control; it's not about personal gain or self-promotion. It's about compassion, love, and the desire to see others lifted up. It's a power that comes from surrender, from recognizing that we don't have all the answers, but that there is a greater force at work, ready to step into our lives and the lives of those around us if we let it.

When a person yields to this greater power, they become a conduit for something miraculous. Their touch can bring healing. Their words can bring life. Their presence can bring peace. The most remarkable thing is that it's not about being a perfect person or having it all figured out. It's about being open to letting this greater power flow through you and trusting that it can change not only your life, but the world around you.

So, how does this affect the world? Imagine a ripple in a pond. When a stone is dropped into the water, it creates ripples that move outward, affecting everything they touch. A person who carries this power into their life becomes like that stone—creating ripples that extend far beyond what they can see. These ripples bring healing, transformation, and hope to others. It's a power that doesn't just stay within; it spreads, touching lives, healing hearts, and transforming communities.

The truth is, when we allow this power to work in us and through us, the world around us cannot remain the same. The tangible effects are seen in the healing of bodies, the restoration of relationships, and the renewal of hope in hearts that were once broken. This is the kind of power that anyone can access, and it has the potential to change the world.

That power, which changes the world around us and brings healing, transformation, and hope, is the very authority we access in Jesus Christ. It's important to understand that this isn't just a vague force or positive energy—it's the power of God Himself, and it's made available to us through Jesus.

When we talk about authority, we're talking about the right and the ability to act. In the natural world, authority is given through position, title, or inheritance. In the spiritual realm, authority comes from being connected to the One who holds all power—Jesus Christ. Through His life, death, and resurrection, Jesus didn't just secure salvation for us; He also opened the way for us to walk in the same authority He had on earth.

You see, during His ministry, Jesus wasn't just performing miracles for the sake of showing power. Every healing, every deliverance, every miracle was a demonstration of the authority He carried from His relationship with the Father. And here's the incredible part: Jesus passed that authority on to us. He said to His followers, "All authority in heaven and on earth has been given to me. Therefore, go…" (Matthew 28:18-19). He commissioned His disciples to go out and continue the work He started, to heal the sick, cast out demons, and proclaim the good news. But He didn't expect them to do it in their own strength; He gave them His authority to carry out that mission.

When we place our faith in Jesus, we're not only forgiven and made new, but we also receive the authority that He has. We're given the right to stand in the same power that raised Him from the dead, and to see that power at work in our lives and in the world around us. This authority isn't something we earn or achieve; it's a gift, made possible by what Jesus accomplished on the cross.

What does that look like practically? It means that when we pray for someone to be healed, we're not just hoping that something might happen. We're standing in the authority of Jesus, knowing that He has already conquered sickness, sin, and death. It means that when we speak peace into a chaotic situation, we're not just offering words of comfort; we're declaring the peace of Christ over that situation, knowing that He has authority over every storm. When we step into dark and broken places, we're not overwhelmed by what we see because we know that we carry the light of Christ, and His authority dispels the darkness.

This authority is not based on our ability or our righteousness; it's based entirely on who Jesus is and what He has done. When He died on the cross, He didn't just defeat sin; He defeated every power of darkness that stands against God's purposes. When He rose from the dead, He declared once and for all that He is victorious, and He invites us to live and act in that victory.

To access this authority, it requires faith. Faith in Jesus is the key that unlocks this power. It's not about how strong our faith is but in whom our faith rests. When we place our trust in Jesus, we are positioned to receive and walk in His authority. We can pray boldly, knowing that we are backed by the power of heaven. We can act courageously, knowing that we are not relying on our own strength but on the strength of the One who holds all things together.

So, when we talk about this tangible power that can change the world around us, we're talking about the authority of Jesus Christ. It's His name that brings healing. It's His power that transforms lives. It's His presence that drives out fear and darkness. And it's His victory that allows us to walk in freedom and confidence, knowing that He is with us and that His authority works through us. This is not just a concept; it's a reality for every believer who puts their trust in Jesus.

GOOD NEWS

There's a powerful idea at the heart of Christian faith, an idea that goes beyond just believing in God or following a set of moral guidelines. It's the belief that someone is always on your side, even when you don't realize it. Imagine for a moment that someone cares so deeply about you that they're constantly thinking of you, wishing the best for you, and, more than that, are actively working behind the scenes on your behalf—helping you in ways you might not ever see.

This isn't just about a human friend or a family member. The Christian message tells us that God Himself is on our side—not in a vague or distant way, but in a personal, close way. You see, the core of the Christian faith is the belief that God loves every person, not just as part of humanity but as individuals. He knows you by name, knows your struggles, your pains, your hopes, and your dreams.

Here's where the message gets truly amazing: God didn't just stay at a distance, hoping we'd somehow find our way to Him. He made a way for us to connect with Him through Jesus Christ. According to Christian belief, Jesus came to earth to bridge the gap between us and God. He lived a life of compassion and grace, showing what it truly means to love others, and ultimately, He gave His life for us. The Bible teaches that through Jesus' life, death, and resurrection, He made it possible for us to experience God's love, forgiveness, and the kind of life we were always meant to live.

Now, you might wonder, "What does that have to do with me?" Well, the Christian faith offers this: No matter where you find yourself in life, no matter what you've been through, or even how far you think you might be from God—He's always there, ready to come alongside you. He's willing to carry the weight of your burdens, to help you through your struggles, and to give you a sense of peace that transcends whatever you're facing.

This isn't just about asking for help in moments of crisis. It's about knowing that, every day, God is with you. He's offering to stand between you and the overwhelming pressures of life, to be your strength, to give you hope, and to bring healing where there's brokenness.

The Christian message is simple: God is for you. He's made a way for you to experience His love through Jesus, and His desire is to walk with you through every aspect of your life. You don't have to carry the weight of the world on your shoulders. There is a God who is willing to carry it for you, who desires to bring healing, peace, and hope into your life.

The invitation is open. All it takes is a simple step of faith—a willingness to reach out, to believe that there's more to life than just what you see, and to trust that God's love is real, available, and personal.

Chapter 1

LIVING IN UNION WITH GOD – THE FOUNDATION OF ALL INTERCESSION

Intercession isn't merely a task; it's the outflow of God's life within you. It begins in the place where **you and the Almighty become one**. This isn't distant, formal prayer—it's intimate, **Spirit-born communion**. The key to all effective prayer is this: Christ alive in you, and you alive in Him. Intercession is not a technique—it's the product of union with God, a life consumed by the fire of His Spirit. When you walk in communion with God, **your prayers carry the weight of heaven** because you have touched the heart of the Father.

The intercessor must live from this place of abiding—anything less will drain your soul and render your prayers powerless. It's not your words that move heaven; it's the Spirit of God in you. And the Spirit flows through those who live in **continual fellowship with the Father**. Every intercessor must learn this: prayer is not merely what you do—it's who you are. You become the vessel through which **God's power touches the earth.**

Intercession isn't just about asking for things—it begins with knowing God deeply. Before we can effectively stand in the gap for others, we must first stand in God's presence. This is why Jesus often retreated to lonely places to pray—not out of duty, but out of delight in His relationship with the Father. **Intercession is birthed from intimacy**. It's about being so aligned with God's heart that your prayers echo heaven's desires on earth.

Just as Adam and Eve walked with God in the cool of the garden, we were created for **communion**. This chapter focuses on the essential truth: everything flows from a life of intimacy with God. Without it, intercession becomes hollow, mere words spoken without power. With it, prayer becomes partnership with the living God, where we discern His will and release it.

Intercession Begins in Union

"I have been crucified with Christ, and I no longer live, but Christ lives in me" (Galatians 2:20).

The power of intercession doesn't come from striving or many words—it comes from **union with God**. It is Christ in you, praying through you. Many try to pray without first entering the presence of God, and they wonder why their prayers lack effect. They pray from their heads instead of their spirits. But real intercession begins when the **Spirit of God takes hold of you**, and you pray from a place of oneness with Him.

The greatest intercessor is not the one who prays the most words, but the one who operates in the Spirit of God. Jesus said, *"The Father and I are one"* (John 10:30). This is the key to intercession—**oneness**. When you abide in God, your spirit and His Spirit move together, and your prayers become His prayers. You are no longer pleading with God—you are releasing His will on earth.

True intercession flows from union with God. The intercessor doesn't beg—he declares, because he knows the will of the Father.

"Your kingdom come, Your will be done, on earth as it is in heaven". (Matthew 6:10).

Communion teaches us to align our hearts with God's will. **Intercession is not aboutpersuading God** to do something He doesn't want to do—it's about partnering with Him to release what is already in His heart.

Jesus is our perfect model of intercession. In John 5:19, He says, *"The Son can do nothing by himself; he can do only what he sees his Father doing."* Effective intercession begins with this same posture—**listening to God before speaking to Him**. Our role as intercessors is to become attuned to His heart and release it through prayer.

This alignment with God's heart often requires stillness and listening. **Intercession starts with being silent before God** and asking, "What is on Your heart today?" The deeper your communion with God, the more accurately your prayers reflect His will.

Becoming a Friend of God

"He who dwells in the secret place of the Most High shall abide under the shadow of the Almighty"(Psalm 91:1).

Every intercessor must learn to dwell in the **secret place of God's presence**. This is where His power is born in you. It's not enough to visit God occasionally—you must learn to live in Him. There is no shortcut to effective intercession. You must become a person saturated with the Holy Spirit. Prayer apart from the presence of God is lifeless. But prayer born from the fire of

His presence will shake nations. "The Lord would speak to Moses face to face, as one speaks to a friend" (Exodus 33:11).

One of the most powerful pictures of communion is the relationship between Moses and God. Moses wasn't just a servant—he was called a friend of God. Intercessors are called to this same intimacy, where prayer is not just a duty but a conversation between friends.

Friendship with God shifts the way you pray. You are no longer praying as a stranger but as someone who knows and trusts Him. The more you grow in friendship with God, the more your heart will naturally align with His, and **intercession will become a joy rather than a burden.**

When Moses came down from the mountain, his face shone with the glory of God. He had been in the presence of the Almighty, and it transformed him. This is what happens to the intercessor who dwells with God—you carry His presence with you, and when you speak, heaven moves. Prayer becomes the outflow of that encounter.

Friendship with God also gives you the boldness to pray big prayers. When you know God's heart and character, you pray with the confidence of a friend who knows that God delights in answering.

To give you an Illustration: Imagine a trusted friend asking you for help. Because of your relationship, you wouldn't hesitate to respond. In the same way, God responds to the prayers of those who know Him intimately.

The Authority of the Intercessor

"You shall receive power when the Holy
Spirit has come upon you" (Acts 1:8).

Authority in prayer is not a theory—it's a reality. The intercessor carries authority because he carries the Spirit of God within him. Jesus said, *"All authority in heaven and on earth has been given to me"* (Matthew 28:18), and that authority flows through you. When you pray from a place of union, your words carry weight because they are backed by authority.

Many intercessors pray as if they are trying to convince God to act. But true intercession isn't begging—it's **declaring what the Spirit has already spoken**. When you know the heart of God, you don't plead—you proclaim. This kind of prayer releases power because it is born from the Spirit's authority, not human effort.

The intercessor prays not as a beggar but as a son or daughter, seated with Christ in heavenly places.

Walking in Communion Every Moment

"Abide in Me, and I in you. As the branch cannot bear fruit of itself, unless it abides in the vine, neither can you, unless you abide in Me" (John 15:4).

Communion with God is not a Sunday experience or a morning devotion—it is a **continuous relationship**. You walk with Him, speak with Him, listen to Him all day long. This is where true intercession happens—in the ordinary moments of life, in the midst of work, rest, and conversation. You become a person who is always praying, always listening, always connected to the Spirit.

Brother Lawrence called this "practicing the presence of God," and it is the foundation of intercession. You don't need perfect conditions to pray. You don't need silence or solitude—you just need Him. Whether you're walking down the street, washing dishes, or facing trials, your heart remains anchored in God's presence. **Prayer becomes the constant undercurrent of your life.**

Practical Steps for a Life of Communion

1. Begin every day by yielding to the Holy Spirit.
  - Before you speak a word, surrender your heart and invite Him to move through you. "Here I am, God—I am listening."

2. Use Scripture to engage with God.
  - Open the Scriptures and let His Word shape your prayers. Scripture is a doorway into communion with Him.

3. Cultivate stillness before God.
  - Make time to sit quietly in His presence. You'll hear more from the Spirit in stillness than in noise.

4. Turn interruptions into opportunities.
  - When life gets busy, don't stop praying—shift your heart toward God and let every moment become a prayer.

5. End each day in thanksgiving.
- Reflect on God's goodness and thank Him for how He moved, even in unseen ways.

Communion as a Place of Transformation

Intercession isn't just about changing situations—it's also about allowing God to change you. When you spend time in God's presence, you become more like Him. His heart becomes your heart. His love for others begins to shape how you see them, and you find yourself praying with compassion and faith.

This is the true power of intercession: it transforms both the person praying and the situation being prayed for. In communion with God, He works within you, conforming you to the image of Christ. Prayer is not just a tool for changing the world—it's a place where God changes us.

Communion with God is the wellspring of all effective intercession. If you want to pray powerfully, begin by dwelling in His presence. Don't rush into prayer—linger with God. Let your heart be shaped by His love, your will aligned with His, and your prayers will carry the weight of heaven's authority.

Intercession Flows from the Spirit Within

True intercession isn't something you strive to do—it's something you become. It is the **natural outflow of a life yielded to the Spirit**. When you walk in communion with God, your prayers carry His authority, His heart, and His power. You pray not as someone on the outside looking in, but as someone seated in Christ, praying from His victory.

This is where intercession becomes powerful—not because of many words, but because of a life surrendered to the Spirit. **Live in communion with God**, and your prayers will move mountains, not by your strength but by His Spirit flowing through you.

The next chapter will build on this foundation, exploring how our identity in Christ gives us authority in intercession. But never forget— **authority comes from intimacy**. Abide in Him, and you will pray with power.

Chapter 2

AUTHORITY IN INTERCESSION – PRAYING FROM YOUR POSITION IN CHRIST

Seated with Christ in Heavenly Places

A ll effective intercession flows from one central truth: you have been given authority in Christ. When Jesus rose from the grave, He not only defeated sin, death, and the powers of darkness—He also gave His victory to those who believe in Him. You have been raised with Christ and **seated with Him in heavenly places** (Ephesians 2:6). This is not a future promise; it's a present reality. You are already seated with Him in the spiritual realm, operating from a place of authority.

Many believers pray as though they are still trying to reach God, as if they are distant beggars rather than beloved sons and daughters. But intercession is not about striving; it's about **praying from your position in Christ**. When you understand where you are seated—with Christ at the right hand of the Father—your prayers take on power, because you pray from **heaven to earth**, not earth to heaven.

The Believer's Identity in Christ

"If anyone is in Christ, he is a new creation. The old has gone, the new is here!" (2 Corinthians 5:17).

Your identity begins with knowing **who you are in Christ**. You are no longer a sinner striving to reach God; you are a new creation, born of His Spirit. The Spirit of Christ now dwells in you, and because of that, you carry His authority. When you pray, you are not merely offering requests—you are exercising the rights of a son or daughter of God.

"We are not trying to pray our way into victory. We are praying from the victory Christ has already won." - Unknown

Many believers pray as though they are still in bondage, but Jesus didn't just forgive your sins—He made you **one with Him**. You are clothed in His righteousness, empowered by His Spirit, and given access to the Father. You have His authority because you are in Him.

The practical takeaway here is to stop praying as though you are distant from God. You are **in Christ**, and Christ is in you. You don't need to fight to get into His presence—you are already there.

Authority through Union with Christ

"All authority in heaven and on earth has been given to me. Therefore, go..." (Matthew 28:18-19).

When Christ gave His disciples the **Great Commission**, He did so with the full weight of His authority. That same authority now rests on every believer who abides in Him. But authority in intercession is not about shouting louder or trying harder—it flows from your union with Christ. When you abide in Him, you speak with the authority of heaven.

Consider how Jesus interceded: He spoke to storms, commanded demons, and healed the sick with a word of authority. He didn't beg or plead—He declared the will of the Father with confidence. And the same Spirit that raised Christ from the dead now lives in you (Romans 8:11). **You have His authority. Use it.**

You are not standing before God as a beggar, but as an ambassador of Christ, representing His kingdom on earth.

Imagine a police officer directing traffic. The authority doesn't come from the officer's personal strength but from the **badge they carry**, representing the government behind them. In the same way, your authority in prayer is not based on your efforts—it's based on Christ's authority in you.

The Role of Faith in Exercising Authority

"Whatever you ask in prayer, believe that you have received it, and it will be yours" (Mark 11:24).

Authority in intercession requires faith. It's not enough to know your position in Christ intellectually—you must believe it with every fiber of your being. **Faith activates the authority you carry**. When you pray in faith, you are not hoping something might happen—you are declaring what is already true in the spiritual realm. Faith sees beyond the natural into the unseen and pulls down heaven's reality into the earth.

But too often, believers are crippled by doubt. They pray without expecting anything to change. This is not the kind of prayer that shifts nations or breaks strongholds. Real intercession prays with faith, expecting God to move. Faith doesn't ask, "Will God do this?" It declares, "God has already made a way."

When you pray from a place of faith, not doubt, declare God's promises with boldness, knowing that **heaven backs your words**. If Christ is in you, there is no room for fear or uncertainty in your prayers.

Authority over Darkness and Strongholds

"The weapons of our warfare are not carnal, but mighty through God to the pulling down of strongholds" (2 Corinthians 10:4).

When you pray from your position in Christ, you have **authority over the works of the enemy**. Jesus didn't just defeat sin—He disarmed the principalities and powers, making a public spectacle of them (Colossians 2:15). That victory is now yours to enforce. When you encounter opposition, you don't shrink back—you stand firm in the authority of Christ and command darkness to flee.

Many believers pray timid prayers when facing spiritual opposition, but Jesus has already given you power over the enemy. You don't need to fear the **devil—the devil fears the Christ in you**. Use the authority you've been given to bind the works of darkness and release God's kingdom.

Picture a soldier who has been given the best weapons and armor. If that soldier doesn't know how to use them, the enemy will still have the upper hand, even though the soldier has superior firepower. The same is true for believers—if you don't exercise your authority, you give the enemy room to operate.

In your intercession, bind the works of darkness and release the will of God. You are **armed with spiritual weapons**—use them.

Practical Ways to Pray with Authority

1. Declare God's promises in prayer.

- Pray Scripture with boldness, knowing that God's Word will not return void (Isaiah 55:11).

2. Use the name of Jesus with faith.

- The name of Jesus carries power over every situation. Speak His name boldly in prayer.

3. Command darkness to flee.

- When facing opposition, don't beg—command the enemy to leave in the authority of Christ.

4. Partner with the Holy Spirit.

- Ask the Holy Spirit to reveal how to pray in each situation. He will guide you into prayers that carry power.

5. Pray with persistence.

- Authority doesn't mean instant results. Keep praying until you see the breakthrough.

Pray from Victory, Not for Victory

You are not an outsider trying to convince God to move. **You are His ambassador**, seated with **Christ, carrying His authority**. When you pray from this position, your words carry the weight of heaven. Intercession is not begging—it is declaring the will of God with the authority of Christ.

Remember this: **authority flows from your position in Christ**. Pray from where you are seated—with Him in heavenly places—and watch as **heaven moves earth through your intercession.**

Chapter 3

THE PRACTICE OF THE PRESENCE OF GOD – A LIFE OF UNCEASING PRAYER

Prayer as a Way of Life

Brother Lawrence, a 17th-century monk, taught that prayer is not limited to set times of devotion—it is a **continuous awareness of God's presence in every moment**. In his classic work, *The Practice of the Presence of God*, Lawrence shows that the highest form of prayer is to live constantly in communion with God, no matter what task is at hand.

For intercessors, this truth is essential. **Intercession is not merely an activity—it's a lifestyle of abiding**. Just as Brother Lawrence found God in the simplicity of washing dishes and cooking meals, you too can learn to dwell in His presence throughout the rhythms of your daily life. This chapter explores what it means to develop the habit of practicing the presence of God and how it transforms intercession from something we "do" to something we become.

Intercession is not just an act or a moment of prayer—it is the lifestyle of one who **walks continually in the presence of God**. The life of an intercessor isn't compartmentalized between "prayer times" and "everyday life." True intercession flows out of **unceasing communion with God**, where every moment is touched by His Spirit.

Prayer in the Ordinary Moments

Brother Lawrence discovered that he could commune with God just as intimately while performing mundane tasks as during moments of structured prayer. He saw no separation between sacred and secular work. Every action, whether scrubbing pots or singing in the chapel, became an offering to God. This insight is life-changing for intercessors: **you don't need perfect conditions to pray**.

In fact, some of the most powerful intercession happens in the midst of life's interruptions—while driving to work, caring for children, or doing chores. **God is present in every moment,** waiting for us to acknowledge Him. When we learn to practice His presence, prayer becomes as natural as breathing. Every conversation, every step, and every task can be filled with the awareness of His nearness.

"Pray without ceasing." (1 Thessalonians 5:17)

This command is not about spending hours on your knees but about learning to **stay connected with God**, even in the most ordinary moments. Intercession becomes not an event but a lifestyle—a continuous dialogue with the One who lives within you.

Many believers compartmentalize their relationship with God. They pray in the morning, then go about their day as if God stays behind. But practicing the presence means **carrying God with you into every situation**. It means praying without ceasing—not by constantly speaking, but by keeping your heart connected to the Spirit throughout the day.

Abiding in God's Love Throughout the Day

Brother Lawrence wrote, *"We should establish ourselves in a sense of God's presence by continually conversing with Him."* This is more than speaking words—it's about **remaining aware of God's love** as you go about your day. When your heart is rooted in the love of God, your prayers naturally align with His will.

Jesus emphasized the importance of abiding: *"Abide in me, and I in you. As the branch cannot bear fruit by itself, unless it abides in the vine, neither can you, unless you abide in me"* (John 15:4). Abiding is the foundation of **fruitful intercession**. As you remain connected to God's heart, you begin to pray from a place of peace, not striving. Your prayers flow from love and trust, not anxiety.

Brother Lawrence learned to return to God repeatedly throughout the day. Whenever his mind wandered, he gently refocused his thoughts on the Lord. This practice teaches us that **intercession is not about perfection.** We will get distracted, but the goal is to return to God quickly and often.

> *"Whatever you do, work heartily, as for the*
> *Lord and not for men."(Colossians 3:23)*

Brother Lawrence found that the **Spirit of God can transform even the most menial tasks** into acts of prayer. When your heart is tuned to God's presence, ordinary work becomes sacred. Washing dishes becomes an act of worship, and walking down the street becomes a time of intercession.

Think of a musician carrying a melody in their heart all day. They may not always be singing aloud, but the song is always playing within them. This is what it means to pray without ceasing—**your spirit remains in tune with God**, even when your hands are busy.

Ask the Holy Spirit to make your work and routines a place of prayer. As you go about your day, whisper prayers, sing in your heart, and listen for His leading. Let the Spirit flow through every action you take.

Turning Every Thought into Prayer

Brother Lawrence once said, *"There is not in the world a kind of life more sweet and delightful than that of a continual conversation with God."* This continual conversation is the heart of intercession. It means bringing every thought, every concern, and every desire before God in **real time**.

You don't need to wait for a prayer meeting to pray for someone or bring a burden to God. The moment a thought enters your mind, it becomes an opportunity for intercession. If someone's name comes to you while driving, pause to pray. If you encounter a challenge at work, invite God into that moment. Intercession becomes seamless when you **turn every thought into prayer**.

This also cultivates sensitivity to the Holy Spirit. When you are constantly aware of God's presence, you become more attuned to His promptings. The Spirit may nudge you to pray for a specific person or situation throughout the day. As you respond in prayer, you are **partnering with heaven in real-time intercession.**

The Joy of Simple Prayers

One of Brother Lawrence's most profound teachings is the **simplicity of prayer**. He believed that short, sincere prayers were just as powerful as long, formal ones. He would lift his heart to God with simple phrases like, "Lord, I am all Yours," or "Help me, Lord."

Many intercessors fall into the trap of thinking that their prayers need to be long and elaborate to be effective. But **God responds to faith, not length**. A brief prayer spoken from the heart can have great power. Brother Lawrence shows us that it's not the words that matter but the **awareness of God's presence** behind them. When you pray with a heart fully connected to God, even the simplest prayer becomes powerful.

"Do not be quick with your mouth, do not be hasty in your heart to utter anything before God. God is in heaven and you are on earth, so let your words be few." (Ecclesiastes 5:2)

Imagine a child who simply rests in their father's arms. They don't need to say much—their presence alone brings joy to their father. This is what God desires from us. When we rest in Him, He delights in us, and our prayers carry His heartbeat.

Practical Steps for Practicing the Presence of God

1. Start your day by inviting God into every moment.

- Before your feet hit the floor in the morning, say, *"Lord, be with me today. I give this day to You."*

- This simple prayer sets the tone for remaining aware of God throughout the day.

2. Use triggers to remind you to pray.
- Choose activities or moments in your routine—like washing dishes, driving, or walking—to consciously turn your heart toward God.
- Each time the task arises, pause and pray, even if briefly.

3. Gently return to God when distracted.
- Don't be discouraged when your mind drifts. Simply refocus and say, *"Here I am again, Lord."* The goal is consistency, not perfection.

4. Pray short, simple prayers throughout the day.
- Whisper a short prayer whenever someone comes to mind: *"Lord, bless them."*
- Over time, this practice will become second nature, and you'll find yourself praying almost without effort.

5. Cultivate gratitude as a form of prayer.
- Thank God for small blessings throughout the day—a kind word, a good meal, or a moment of peace. **Gratitude keeps your heart open to His presence.**

A Life Lived with God

Brother Lawrence's life reminds us that **intercession is not confined to specific times or places**—it is a way of being. When you practice the presence of God, prayer becomes the air you breathe. You carry His presence with you into every moment, and every moment becomes an opportunity to pray, to worship, and to stand in the gap for others.

The joy of practicing His presence is that **you are never alone.** Whether washing dishes, commuting to work, or sitting in silence, God is with you. And as you remain aware of His presence, your heart becomes a wellspring of intercession. You'll find yourself praying effortlessly, moved by the Spirit, releasing God's purposes into the world with simplicity and joy.

This is the beauty of intercession: **It's not something you have to "do"—it's something you become**. The intercessor who practices God's presence lives in continuous communion, always listening, always praying, and always abiding. From this place of unceasing prayer, you will carry heaven's authority with grace and peace, transforming the world around you one moment at a time.

The next chapter will explore how to partner with the Holy Spirit in discerning God's will in intercession. But remember—it all begins here: **live in His presence, and intercession will flow naturally.**

Chapter 4

PARTNERING WITH THE HOLY SPIRIT – THE INTERCESSOR'S GUIDE TO SUPERNATURAL PRAYER

The Spirit Prays Through Us

The life of an intercessor is not about praying according to human understanding but **partnering with the Holy Spirit**, who knows the mind of God and the needs of the moment. The Spirit doesn't merely assist us in prayer—He prays through us, aligning our hearts with the will of God.

True intercession is not human effort; it is **divine partnership**. The Spirit fills, leads, and empowers us to pray beyond our own knowledge.

Romans 8:26 tells us that the Spirit helps us in our weakness, interceding through us with groanings too deep for words. This means there will be times when your natural mind cannot grasp the fullness of what needs to be prayed, but the Spirit will pray through you with precision and power. Yielding to His guidance is essential for effective intercession.

The Holy Spirit: The Source of Supernatural Insight

"The Spirit searches all things, even the
deep things of God." (1 Corinthians 2:10)

The Holy Spirit gives intercessors access to the **mind and heart of God**. There are things that only God knows—hidden struggles, future events, and the spiritual roots of issues. It is through the Spirit's leading that the intercessor becomes aware of these unseen realities. Without the Spirit, our prayers are limited. But with the Spirit, we can pray with divine insight.

The Holy Spirit will often reveal specific people, places, or issues that need prayer. He may bring someone to mind during your day or impress a situation upon your heart. These impressions are not random—they are **invitations to intercede**. As you respond to the Spirit's prompting, you align with the purposes of heaven.

Imagine tuning a radio to the right frequency. When your spirit is tuned to the Holy Spirit, you receive His signals clearly. In the same way, the Spirit tunes your heart to the will of God so that your prayers **hit the mark**.

A mentor and friend, Chad Dedmon, once was in prayer and was presented with Something. It was an image of a man listening to specific music and contemplating taking his own life. This was something God showed him seemingly out of nowhere. Chad didn't shrug it off or ignore it but began to pray in the Spirit and pray over the man and his life. That Sunday, he happened to run into a kind of confused-looking person outside the church, and it was his first time there. As they got to talking, the man opened up about some struggles, and Chad realized it was the same guy. He told him the story, and the man was shocked. The details and date and time were exact to when the man had intended to end his own life. He didn't know why he hadn't done it, but something came over him, and he changed his mind. These are the kinds of things that you get to partner with God to see happen. I have countless instances of situations similar to this one where you can't help but be in awe of what God will do.

Pay attention to the Spirit's impressions. If someone or something comes to mind unexpectedly, take a moment to pray—you may be participating in something God is doing.

Praying in the Spirit: Beyond Human Understanding

"Praying always with all prayer and supplication in the Spirit." (Ephesians 6:18)

Praying in the Spirit is essential for powerful intercession. This includes both praying with supernatural insight and praying in tongues. When you pray in tongues, your spirit prays directly to God, bypassing the limitations of your mind. In this form of prayer, the Holy Spirit intercedes through you in alignment with the **perfect will of God** (1 Corinthians 14:2).

When we pray in the Spirit, we go beyond the natural, engaging with God's purposes at a level our minds cannot comprehend.

Praying in the Spirit strengthens you, builds faith, and gives you endurance in prayer. There are situations that cannot be addressed by human words alone—only Spirit-led intercession can get the job done.

Think of intercession as a deep well. Your human understanding can only draw water from the surface, but the Spirit reaches into the depths of God's wisdom and brings forth what is needed in that moment.

Discernment and Spiritual Warfare in Intercession

"For we are not unaware of his schemes." (2 Corinthians 2:11)

Partnering with the Holy Spirit enables intercessors to discern the strategies of the enemy and engage in effective spiritual warfare. Intercession is not merely asking for blessings—it is **enforcing the victory of Christ over darkness**. The Spirit equips intercessors with discernment to recognize spiritual opposition and break strongholds through prayer.

There will be times when the Spirit reveals hindrances, demonic attacks, or spiritual bondage that need to be confronted. The intercessor, armed with the authority of Christ, binds these works of darkness and releases the will of God.

We don't fight for victory—we fight from victory. Christ has already triumphed, and our prayers enforce His reign over every situation.

Picture a watchman on a city wall, alert to any approaching danger. In the same way, the Holy Spirit alerts intercessors to spiritual threats, calling them to action through prayer.

When the Spirit reveals opposition or strongholds, respond immediately. Use your authority in Christ to bind the enemy and declare God's victory.

• **Stay Alert:** Just as a watchman on a city wall stays vigilant, commit to daily prayer, asking the Holy Spirit to sharpen your discernment and reveal spiritual opposition. Be attentive to His nudges and act immediately in prayer when He brings something to your attention.

• **Use Authority:** Remember that Christ has already won the victory. When you sense spiritual opposition, pray with confidence and authority, declaring God's truth and binding the enemy's schemes. Speak God's Word over the situation—Scripture is your greatest weapon in spiritual warfare.

• **Prepare:** Put on the full armor of God daily (Ephesians 6:10-18), especially focusing on the Sword of the Spirit (God's Word) and the Shield of Faith. Use these tools actively in intercession, speaking promises of Scripture into the areas of struggle you're led to pray for.

The Spirit of Revelation: Praying According to God's Will

"This is the confidence we have: that if we ask anything according to His will, He hears us." (1 John 5:14)

Effective intercession is not about imposing our desires on God—it is about praying His will into being. But how do we know the will of God? The answer is through the **Spirit of revelation**. The Holy Spirit reveals what is on the heart of the Father, leading us to pray in alignment with His purposes.

This requires listening before speaking. The intercessor must cultivate a sensitive spirit—waiting on God, asking Him what to pray, and responding in obedience. **God's will is not a complete mystery** to the Spirit-filled believer; it is revealed in partnership with the Holy Spirit.

Think of a sailboat catching the wind. The boat's power comes not from the rowers, but from the wind filling its sails. In the same way, intercession is powerful when the Spirit fills your prayers with the **wind of heaven**.

Ask the Holy Spirit to reveal God's will before you pray. Wait in stillness and listen for His leading. Your prayers will become more effective as you align with heaven's purposes.

The Spirit's Role in Manifestation

"When Zion travailed, she brought forth her children." (Isaiah 66:8)

There are moments in intercession when the Spirit moves you into travail—deep, Spirit-led prayer that births what God has promised. Just as a mother labors to bring forth life, the intercessor labors in prayer until God's purposes are brought to pass. **Travail is not human effort—it is the Spirit groaning through us**.

This type of prayer can be intense, marked by tears, groanings, and deep emotion. It is a sign that something is being birthed in the Spirit. As you yield to the Spirit in these moments, **breakthroughs are released**—in families, churches, nations, and individuals.

Consider Elijah on Mount Carmel, praying for rain after a long drought. He labored in prayer seven times, sending his servant to check the horizon until a small cloud appeared. Similarly, travailing prayer requires persistence until the manifestation comes.

When the Spirit leads you into travail, don't hold back. Allow the Spirit to pray through you, and continue until you see the answer.

Becoming a Vessel of the Spirit's Power

Partnering with the Holy Spirit in intercession transforms ordinary prayer into a **divine encounter with power and revelation**. As you yield to the Spirit, your prayers will go beyond human wisdom, touching the heart of God and shifting spiritual realities.

The intercessor is not merely a petitioner; they are a **co-laborer with God**, empowered by His Spirit to move in power.

In the next chapter, we will explore the role of persistence in prayer—how to press through opposition and delay until God's promises are fulfilled. But remember this: **Every powerful intercessor is first a vessel of the Holy Spirit**. Let the Spirit lead, and you will pray with precision, power, and purpose.

Chapter 5

THE HEALING POWER OF GOD – MANIFESTING TODAY THROUGH INTERCESSION

The God Who Heals is the Same Yesterday, Today, and Forever

*J*esus is still the Healer today. *The same power that healed the sick and raised the dead in the days of the apostles is available to every believer now. The power of God to heal has never diminished, only our faith and understanding of it has.*

God's nature is unchanging—**He is still the Healer**. What He did through Jesus and the apostles, He is still doing today. **Divine healing** is not confined to a specific period in church history—it is a reality that believers can experience and manifest today. This chapter will explore the **continuing power of God to heal**, how believers can step into that power, and how to heal in faith.

John G. Lake is a notable figure in our church history. His life was marked by the manifestation of God's healing power. He believed that **healing was not only possible but a guarantee for those who placed their faith in God's promises.** In this chapter, we will explore the foundations of

healing, the role of faith and intercession, and how the healing ministry of
Jesus continues through His church today.

I remember as a young kid at Metro Church in Kansas City there
was an Elder named Don James. He is one of the most genuine and kind
hearted people I have ever met. He was a woodworker as a hobby and had
an accident with a saw. He lost the ends of most of the fingers on his right
hand. Unfortunately some were below the knuckle and were not expected to
grow back. I insisted on praying for him each week and this continued long
after this incident. Not only did his fingers grow, it actually led to more pain
because his fingernails eventually began to form under the surface of his
skin. Something else that I was told was not supposed to happen. Especially
for a man who was in his late 60s at the time.

It was God's healing power that initially set me on my journey of
intercession. I was 17 and worked as a lifeguard at the YMCA. One day some
of the lifeguards were playing around and running in and out of the office.
There was a big metal door between the office and pool area and when one
of the lifeguards let go of it, the result was that it opened way to quickly onto
the other guards foot. That lifeguards' name was Hannah and she has been a
friend of mine for as long as I can remember.

The metal door had taken off Hannahs' big toenail. Thankfully, being
lifeguards, we had first aid supplies on hand. We bandaged it up and Hannah
took fifteen minutes or so to recover. When she returned she was sitting on
the stand and complaining about the pain she was in.

To be fully transparent, my life wasn't easy at the time. I was going
through a lot and was fairly preoccupied with myself. This is already fairly
common among teenagers. All of this was to say that, while I did truly care
that my friend was hurt, I could have definitely been more compassionate
and empathetic at the time. I was stuck at work and had no other way to help
her any further. She was still saying she was in pain so in an effort to get her
to stop complaining, I offered to pray for it. I did not expect her to accept my
offer. She said yes, so there I was, stuck having to publicly pray for someone
like we were in church or something. I simply asked if God could heal her
toe and said I know that Jesus healed people in the Bible and God can do
anything. It was a short simple prayer. To my surprise, she said her toe was

better. She looked a little confused as she was processing it. Her pain had instantly left. The pussing and bleeding stopped at the same moment.

Hannah was a long distance runner and had a state level cross country meet that coming weekend. She had been thinking she would have to drop out but because of the improvement she was able to continue training and compete.

I had visited my parents church at the time and knew they at least touched on the concept of healing. I began attending there, Harmony Vineyard, and that's where I met Ryan Snow, a youth pastor who completely revolutionized my understanding of God's will to heal. Eventually a youth leader Thomas Devick took a group of us to a training that was run by the John G Lake ministry. Things only took off after that. Many of us were seeing miracle after miracle. It got to a point that I was receiving phone call requests to come pray for the sick at home or in the hospital. I was asked to share the testimony of what God was doing with the entire church of a couple thousand people one Sunday as well.

Healing is God's Will Today

"I am the Lord who heals you." (Exodus 15:26)

The foundation of all prayer for healing must rest on the unshakable truth that **healing is the will of God**. Throughout Scripture, God reveals Himself as **Yahweh Rapha—the Lord who heals. Jesus'** ministry was marked by constant healing, and He demonstrated that **God's will is to heal all who come to Him in faith**.

"The question is not whether God wants to heal, but whether we are ready to believe and pray to see healing manifest."

John G Lake would often say that **healing was as much a part of Christ's atonement as forgiveness of sins**. He believed and taught that healing is available to all through faith in Jesus' finished work. **Faith in God's will to heal is the first step** toward seeing miracles manifest today.

Begin every prayer for healing with confidence that it is God's will to heal. Align your prayers with the truth that God's healing power is available today, just as it was in the days of Jesus.

Faith and Healing: The Key to Receiving God's Power

"Your faith has made you well." (Matthew 9:22)

Healing is received through **faith**. Throughout the gospels, Jesus continually emphasized that **faith was the key** to unlocking healing. **Faith is not merely hope—it is the conviction that God's power to heal is real and available**. For healing to manifest, faith must be present, both in the one receiving the healing and in those interceding on their behalf.

"Faith is the hand that reaches into the unseen and pulls the power of God into the seen realm. Without faith, healing remains inaccessible—but with faith, nothing is impossible."

In Lake's healing ministry, he witnessed **thousands of miraculous healings** by placing an unwavering emphasis on faith. **He would often pray with people for hours, days, or even weeks, declaring that God's power would manifest as they continued to believe**. He taught that **persistence in faith was key for healing** in cases where the answer didn't come instantly.

Pray with unwavering faith for healing, knowing that God's power is ready to manifest. Teach those who are receiving prayer to hold onto faith, even if the healing process takes time.

The Role of Intercession in Releasing God's Healing Power

"And the prayer of faith will save the sick, and the Lord will raise him up." (James 5:15)

Intercession plays a vital role in healing. Many healings throughout the Bible and church history were the result of **persistent intercessory prayer**.

When we pray for healing, we are not pleading with God to heal—He already desires to heal. We are enforcing the victory of Jesus over sickness, declaring that healing must manifest because of what Christ has done.

Lake often gathered **groups of intercessors** to pray for the sick, especially when he was dealing with large numbers of people in need of healing. He saw **corporate intercession** as a way to **build up the faith of the body** and **release a greater anointing for healing**. Many of the miracles that marked his ministry were birthed out of **hours of intercessory prayer**.

Incorporate intercession into your healing prayers. Gather others to pray with you for healing, and be persistent in your prayers.

Walking in the Healing Power of God Today

Scripture: *"And these signs will follow those who believe: In My name they will lay hands on the sick, and they will recover." (Mark 16:17-18)*

The healing power of God is not limited to a select few—it is available to **every believer who walks in faith**. Jesus commissioned all believers to **lay hands on the sick and expect them to recover. Healing is part of the believer's inheritance**, and walking in the power of God requires **obedience to His command to heal**.

Healing was never meant to be an isolated occurrence in the church. It is meant to be the norm for every believer, a demonstration of God's kingdom on earth.

Lake was passionate about training others to **walk in the power of God**, particularly in the area of healing. His healing rooms in Spokane, Washington, were not just places for people to receive prayer—they were also **training grounds** where believers learned how to pray for the sick and see God's power released through them.

Step out in faith and pray for healing whenever the opportunity arises. Lay hands on the sick, pray and expect God's healing power to manifest through you.

Healing as a Sign of God's Kingdom on Earth

"But if I cast out demons by the Spirit of God, surely the kingdom of God has come upon you."(Matthew 12:28)

Healing is one of the most powerful signs of the **kingdom of God manifesting in this world**. Every time someone is healed by the power of **God, it is a demonstration that God is present and active. Healing shows that God's power has come to overthrow the works of darkness**, including sickness and disease.

"Healing is not just a gift—it is a manifestation of the kingdom of God on earth. Every time someone is healed, we are witnessing the power of God's kingdom at work."

Lake often spoke of how **healing was a visible demonstration of God's kingdom**. He believed that healings were not just for the benefit of the individual but were a **testimony to the world** that Jesus was alive and His kingdom was advancing. Lake saw healing as a sign that **accompanied the preaching of the gospel**, confirming the reality of God's power.

View healing as a demonstration of God's kingdom. When you pray for healing, recognize that you are manifesting God's kingdom on the earth, pushing back the works of darkness.

Practical Application: Stepping Into Authority

When we talk about healing and transformation through the authority of Jesus Christ, it's important to understand how to practically walk in that authority. Often, we use the word "pray" to describe what we're doing, because it gives the person in front of us a framework for what's happening. While prayer is happening as we are in communion with God, the work we are doing isn't prayer itself. There is not a single instance of Jesus telling the disciples to pray for the sick when He sent them out. He tells them to heal the sick and He sends them with the authority to do it.

Here are the practical steps to take:

1. Command the Sickness or Infirmity to Leave in Jesus' Name

Jesus demonstrated this during His earthly ministry. When He encountered sickness, He didn't beg or plead—He spoke with authority. Follow His example by commanding the sickness to leave, using the name of Jesus. Scripture teaches us that His name carries the ultimate authority:

"Therefore God exalted Him to the highest place and gave Him the name that is above every name" (Philippians 2:9).

Speak directly to the condition, saying something like, *"In the name of Jesus, I command this sickness to leave. I declare that every root of infirmity must go, and I release the healing power of Jesus into this body."*

2. Speak to the Body and Declare Wholeness

Once you have commanded the sickness to leave, address the person's body. The Bible says, *"By His stripes we are healed"* (Isaiah 53:5) and *"By His wounds you have been healed"* (1 Peter 2:24). These verses affirm that healing was accomplished through the finished work of the cross and the whipping post. Speak wholeness over their body with confidence, declaring the truth of what Jesus has already done:

"I declare that this body is healed and made whole by the finished work of Jesus Christ. By His stripes, you were healed. Every cell, organ, and system in this body must align with the Word of God and function in perfect health."

3. Stand in Faith and Expect Results

After speaking, trust that God is at work. Healing isn't about your strength or words—it's about the power of Jesus and the authority He has given to believers. Faith is the key that unlocks the power of heaven. Believe that the work has been done, even if the results are not immediately visible. Scripture reminds us, *"The prayer of a righteous person is powerful and effective"* (James 5:16).

4. Encourage the Person to Receive and Thank God

Lead the person in thanking God for what He has done. Gratitude is an act of faith that acknowledges God's power and goodness. Encourage them to continue speaking life and truth over themselves, even after the moment of prayer has passed.

Key Scriptures to Use in Authority

• *"By His stripes we are healed"* (Isaiah 53:5).

• *"He Himself bore our sins in His body on the cross, so that we might die to sins and live for righteousness; by His wounds you have been healed"* (1 Peter 2:24).

• *"Truly I tell you, if anyone says to this mountain, 'Go, throw yourself into the sea,' and does not doubt in their heart but believes that what they say will happen, it will be done for them"* (Mark 11:23).

• *"In My name they will drive out demons; they will place their hands on sick people, and they will get well"* (Mark 16:17-18).

By stepping into the authority of Jesus Christ and applying these practical steps, you are not just praying—you are declaring the finished work of the cross and partnering with God to bring healing and restoration into the lives of those around you.

God's Healing Power is Alive and Available Today

The healing power of God is just as real and present today as it was in the days of Jesus. **God has not changed—He is still Yahweh Rapha, the God who heals**. Every believer is called to walk in that healing power, to intercede for the sick, and to expect miraculous healing as a demonstration of God's kingdom on earth. **Healing is not for a select few—it is the inheritance of all who believe**.

The same Spirit that raised Christ from the dead lives in you, and through that Spirit, the healing power of God is available today. Step into it, pray with faith, and watch as the miraculous becomes the norm.

In the next chapter, we will explore how the intercessor's life continues to be transformed by intimacy with God, deepening the well from which they draw in prayer. But remember this: **healing is part of God's plan for today, and you are called to carry that power into the world**.

Chapter 6

PRESSING THROUGH – THE POWER OF PERSISTENCE IN INTERCESSION

The Nature of Prevailing Prayer

The world often expects immediate results, but **prayer is not always answered instantly**. There are times when breakthrough requires persistent, unrelenting intercession. This is **the prayer that refuses to let go until God's promises are fulfilled**.

"*Real faith is not deterred by delay or opposition. It presses on, believing that God is faithful and His word will come to pass.*"

In Luke 18, Jesus gave the parable of the **persistent widow** who kept pleading with an unjust judge until he granted her request. Jesus ended the story by saying: "*Will not God bring justice for His chosen ones who cry out to Him day and night?*" (Luke 18:7) The message is clear—**God responds to persistent prayer**.

This chapter explores **why persistence is necessary**, what obstacles believers must overcome, and how **faith-fueled endurance** in prayer is key with God's promises.

Why Persistence is Required in Intercession

"Ask, and it will be given to you; seek, and you will find; knock, and the door will be opened to you."(Matthew 7:7)

Why does God sometimes delay answers to prayer? One reason is that **God's timing is perfect**—He knows when to release the answer. Another reason is that **spiritual resistance exists**, and persistent prayer breaks through the barriers of darkness. Persistence builds spiritual endurance, strengthens our faith, and draws us closer to God.

Think of rain filling a jar, drop by drop. Each prayer is like a drop—individually, it may not seem to make a difference, but **eventually, the jar overflows**. Many believers stop praying just before the breakthrough comes. **Persistent prayer is the steady stream that fills the jar until the promise overflows into reality**.

The answer is often on the other side of persistence. Don't quit before the miracle.

Recognize that **delay is not denial**. Keep pressing in until you see the breakthrough.

Pressing Through Opposition and Resistance

"From the first day that you set your heart to understand... your words were heard, but the prince of the Persian kingdom resisted me twenty-one days." (Daniel 10:12-13)

In Daniel 10, the angel revealed that **Daniel's prayer was heard the moment he prayed**, but spiritual resistance delayed the answer. This passage shows that **persistent prayer engages in spiritual warfare**. There are times when the enemy resists God's answers, and **it takes endurance in intercession to break through**.

Imagine a miner digging for gold. At first, he finds only dirt and rock, but he keeps digging, knowing the treasure lies beneath. **Intercession works**

the same way. There may be resistance, but the intercessor presses on, knowing the promise is waiting on the other side.

Spiritual warfare requires more than a one-time prayer. It demands persistence until the enemy's grip is broken and God's will is manifested.

When you encounter **spiritual resistance or delay**, don't stop. Press through with the authority of Christ, declaring God's promises over the situation.

The Role of Faith and Patience in Prevailing Prayer

"Through faith and patience, we
inherit the promises." (Hebrews 6:12)

Persistence in prayer requires not only faith but also **patience**. Faith believes that God is faithful to His promises, while patience holds on during the waiting period. Many believers grow weary because they lack patience—they begin to doubt or give up when the answer takes time. But **faith coupled with patience leads to victory**.

Patience is not passive waiting—it is the active posture of trust, standing firm on God's promises.

Think of a farmer who plants seeds. He waters them daily, trusting that the harvest will come, though nothing is visible at first. **Every prayer you pray is like a seed planted in the soil of God's promises**. In due season, the harvest will come, if you don't give up.

Stand firm on God's promises. **Remind yourself of His faithfulness** during the waiting season. The harvest will come.

Persistence Unlocks the Impossible

"Therefore I tell you, whatever you ask for in prayer, believe
that you have received it, and it will be yours." (Mark 11:24)

There are some breakthroughs that will not come **without persistent, bold prayer**. God often tests the strength of our faith—not to withhold

His blessings, but to see if we will stand in faith until the promise comes. Persistent prayer unlocks **doors that appear shut** and moves **mountains that seem immovable**.

Consider Elijah on Mount Carmel, praying for rain after a long drought (1 Kings 18:41-45). **He prayed seven times**, sending his servant to check the sky each time. Finally, a small cloud appeared—an indication that the rain was coming. **If Elijah had quit after six prayers, the breakthrough would never have come**.

Persistence in prayer unlocks doors that would remain shut without faith-filled perseverance.

If the answer seems delayed, **pray again. Then pray again**. Keep knocking until the door opens.

How to Strengthen Yourself for Persistent Prayer

Persistence in prayer can be exhausting if you rely on your own strength. The key is to **stay connected to God and be empowered by His Spirit**. Here are practical ways to maintain endurance:

1. Pray in the Spirit.
- Praying in tongues builds inner strength and refreshes your spirit (Jude 1:20).

2. Meditate on God's promises.
- Keep your faith alive by speaking and meditating on Scriptures that declare God's faithfulness.

3. Find prayer partners.
- Corporate intercession strengthens individual faith. Find others to stand with you in persistent prayer.

4. Worship while you wait.
- Worship keeps your heart connected to God and lifts your eyes off the circumstances.

5. Journal your progress.
- Record answered prayers and small victories along the way to encourage yourself to keep going.

You don't fight in your own strength—God strengthens those who wait on Him.

When you feel weary, **refresh yourself in God's presence**. Lean into the Spirit, who empowers you to keep going.

Refusing to Quit Until the Breakthrough Comes

Persistent prayer is the **hallmark of every great intercessor**. It takes faith, endurance, and the willingness to press through obstacles and delays. But those who refuse to quit will see the promises of God fulfilled. **Breakthrough belongs to those who endure**.

The next chapter will explore **the role of thanksgiving and praise in intercession**—how worship shifts atmospheres and brings manifestation. But remember this: **In God's kingdom, persistence is power**. Keep pressing in.

Chapter 7

THANKSGIVING, PRAISE, AND WORSHIP – UNLOCKING HEAVEN'S POWER IN INTERCESSION

Worship as Spiritual Warfare

Many believers view worship as a prelude to prayer, but in truth, **worship is a weapon**. Through thanksgiving and praise, we align ourselves with the reality of God's victory and **disarm fear, doubt, and opposition**.

Worship is not only for the sanctuary—it is a weapon in the battle. When we lift our praise, the heavens respond, and the powers of darkness are shaken.

Paul and Silas experienced this truth well. **In a prison cell, beaten and shackled, they began to sing hymns of praise to God**. Suddenly, the prison shook, their chains fell off, and the doors opened (Acts 16:25-26). This chapter will explore **how praise and thanksgiving bring breakthrough, silence the enemy, and prepare the way for answered prayer**.

Thanksgiving: Unlocking the Gates of Heaven

"Enter His gates with thanksgiving and
His courts with praise." (Psalm 100:4)

Thanksgiving is **the first step into putting the focus on God**. When we give thanks, we acknowledge God's goodness, faithfulness, and provision, no matter what our circumstances look like. **Thanksgiving is an act of faith**. It shifts our focus from problems to God's promises and brings us into a higher perspective.

A heart filled with thanksgiving has no room for fear or doubt. Gratitude opens the gates of heaven and invites God into every situation.

Picture a locked gate. Thanksgiving is the key that opens the gate and allows you to step into God's perspective. **Gratitude is not a reaction—it is a choice to acknowledge God's goodness even when circumstances are hard.**

Start every prayer with **thanksgiving, even in difficult situations**. Thank God for what He has done and what He will do, knowing that He is working on your behalf.

Praise: Shifting Atmospheres and Breaking Strongholds

"The Lord inhabits the praises of His people." (Psalm 22:3)

Praise is more than singing songs—it is a declaration of God's greatness and power. **When we praise, we invite God into the situation and release His power**. Praise also silences the enemy and breaks spiritual oppression. As we lift our praise, **strongholds are dismantled, and victory is declared**.

The enemy cannot remain where praise rises. Every time you praise, you proclaim the victory of Christ and release the authority of heaven into your circumstances.

Think of King Jehoshaphat's army in 2 Chronicles 20. When they were surrounded by enemies, **God instructed them to put singers at the front**

of the army. As they sang praises to God, their enemies were thrown into confusion, and victory was secured. **Praise was the weapon that won the battle**.

Use praise as a tool in prayer. When you encounter fear, discouragement, or spiritual opposition, begin to praise God. Declare His greatness, and watch the atmosphere shift.

Worship: Aligning with Heaven's Throne Room

"On earth as it is in heaven." (Matthew 6:10)

Worship connects us to the throne room of God. **In heaven, worship never ceases, and every act of worship on earth aligns us with that reality**. When we worship, we are no longer praying from earth to heaven—we are seated with Christ in heavenly places (Ephesians 2:6). Worship shifts our perspective from earthly limitations to heavenly possibilities.

Worship takes us beyond the earthly realm and into the presence of the Most High, where every resource of heaven is available.

Picture Isaiah's vision of God high and exalted (Isaiah 6:1-8). In the presence of God's holiness, Isaiah was transformed and commissioned for his calling. **Worship is not only an encounter—it is a place of commissioning and empowerment**. When we worship, we align with devine purposes and receive strength to fulfill them.

Cultivate a **lifestyle of worship**. Don't limit worship to music—let every moment of your life be an offering to God, aligning your heart with His purposes.

Worship as Warfare: Shutting the Mouth of the Enemy

"From the lips of children and infants, You
have ordained praise because of Your enemies,
to silence the foe and the avenger." (Psalm 8:2)

Worship is a form of spiritual warfare that **silences the enemy**. The enemy thrives on fear, lies, and accusation, but praise and worship disarm him. Every time we lift our voices in worship, we declare that **God is victorious and the enemy is defeated**. Worship shifts the focus from what the enemy is doing to what God has already done through Christ.

Imagine being in a courtroom, where the accuser's voice is loud. But when **the intercessor begins to worship, the Judge rises from His seat, and the accuser is silenced**. Worship reminds the enemy that his defeat is final.

Use worship to silence fear and accusation. When lies try to overwhelm you, respond with worship, declaring God's truth and victory.

Thanksgiving and Praise Prepare the Way

"You are my God, and I will praise You...
You have become my salvation." (Psalm 118:28)

Thanksgiving and praise are **more than responses to victory—they prepare the way for it**. When we praise in faith, even before the answer comes, we create an atmosphere where God's power is present. Faith-filled praise is a declaration that **God's promises are true, even if circumstances say otherwise**.

Praise is not just a response to what God has done—it is a declaration of what He will do.

Remember the walls of Jericho (Joshua 6). **Israel shouted in praise before the walls fell**. Their shout wasn't a celebration of what had happened—it was a declaration of what was about to happen. **Praise declares faith for Gods' will to manifest**.

Praise God before you see the answer. Thank Him, even while you are still waiting for it. Your praise creates the pathway for God's power to be revealed.

Living a Life of Thanksgiving, Praise, and Worship

The intercessor who understands the power of thanksgiving, praise, and worship becomes **a conduit of God's power on earth**. Worship is not just a ritual or a Sunday morning activity—it is **a way of life and a declaration of victory**. As you live a life of worship, **you align yourself with God's purposes, silence the enemy, and prepare the way for God's will to be manifested on Earth.**

Thanksgiving opens the gates, praise shifts the atmosphere, and worship brings you into the throne room of God. In this place, victory is assured.

In the next chapter, we will explore **how prophetic intercession allows believers to declare the future God intends, speaking His promises into existence**. But remember this: **Thanksgiving, praise, and worship are the foundation of every effective intercessor. They allow God's power to be manifested into every situation**.

Chapter 8

PROPHETIC INTERCESSION – DECLARING GOD'S WILL WITH AUTHORITY

The Power of Spoken Prayer

*P*rayer is not a begging exercise. It is not a timid request for God to intervene; it is the believer standing as an ambassador of Christ, declaring His will on earth.

Prophetic intercession is **Spirit-empowered prayer** in which the believer, led by the Holy Spirit, **declares God's will into situations and nations**. It requires a keen ear tuned to heaven and a bold heart willing to decree what God intends, regardless of what circumstances suggest.

Lake's ministry was marked by this kind of intercession—bold declarations of healing, deliverance, and the manifestation of God's power. **Prophetic prayer does not plead; it proclaims**. The intercessor stands in the authority of Christ and speaks to mountains, commanding them to move.

In this chapter, we will explore what it means to **pray prophetically**, how to discern God's will in prayer, and how to release His purposes on earth through faith-filled declarations.

It was 2013 and I found myself with a group of friends in a classroom in Europe. The classroom was made up entirely of students of another faith. I began sharing on some of the miraculous things I had seen. Then a woman named Sherry Colvin who has such a sincere walk with God pointed out a student. She asked if his father was in the hospital at the moment. He answered yes with a shocked look on his face as the rest of the room sat on edge. She asked him if it was something to do with his stomach. He sat there shocked for a moment while the response from the other students in the room confirmed for us that it was correct. The young man then said yes. Sherry went on to explain what she felt God was showing her about their household. She told him that Jesus wants to heal his father and the only reason she was shown those things was because the true and living God wanted to make himself known to them. This situation was obviously something that the other students in the room were very aware of already but it was also clearly something that Sherry had no earthly way of knowing. Roughly 15-20 students all eagerly prayed to invite Jesus into their lives and ask God to continue to make himself known to them. This is just one of many applications that prayer and the prophetic gift can have.

Prophetic Intercession is Partnering with the Holy Spirit

"The Spirit Himself intercedes for us
through wordless groans." (Romans 8:26)

Prophetic intercession begins with **intimacy with the Holy Spirit**. It is not rooted in human wisdom or personal desires—it flows from the heart and mind of God. The intercessor's job is to **listen for the Spirit's leading** and pray what God is declaring. **Prophetic prayer is born out of intimacy with God**, where the intercessor's spirit is aligned with God's purposes.

The intercessor is God's mouthpiece on earth. When the Spirit speaks, you must speak—and the earth will shift at the sound of it.

In Ezekiel 37, God commanded Ezekiel to **prophesy over a valley of dry bones**. When Ezekiel spoke the word of the Lord, the bones came together, and life was restored. **The key was not Ezekiel's eloquence, but his obedience to speak what God had instructed**. Likewise, prophetic intercessors pray what the Spirit reveals, bringing life to dead situations.

Spend time with God, listening to and growing familiar with the Spirit's promptings. **Speak only what the Spirit prompts**, knowing that your words now carry power.

The Authority to Declare God's Will on Earth

"Truly I tell you, whatever you bind on earth will be bound in heaven, and whatever you loose on earth will be loosed in heaven." (Matthew 18:18)

God has given believers **authority to enforce His will on earth**. Prophetic intercession involves **binding the plans of the enemy and releasing God's purposes**. This is not wishful thinking or hopeful praying— it is **exercising authority**.

God does not merely intervene from heaven; He works through men and women who will speak His word with authority. As ambassadors of Christ, we have been given the power to loose His will and bind what opposes it.

John G Lake often told stories of confronting sickness with bold declarations of healing. He did not plead with God to act—**he commanded the sickness to leave, knowing that God had already given authority over it**. In the same way, prophetic intercessors must **pray with confidence**, knowing that God's promises are true and His power is available.

Speak with authority. When you pray, declare God's promises over situations and confront the works of the enemy with the authority of Christ.

Declaring God's Promises Before They Manifest

"God, who gives life to the dead and calls into being things that were not." (Romans 4:17)

Faith-filled intercession **declares what God has promised even before it is visible**. The world waits for evidence, but the **intercessor**

speaks by faith, knowing that God's word is more reliable than any earthly circumstance.

Faith is the hand that reaches into the future and pulls God's promise into the present.

In 1 Kings 18, Elijah declared, *"There is the sound of a heavy rain,"* even though there was no cloud in the sky. **Elijah's prophetic declaration preceded the manifestation of the rain**. Similarly, prophetic intercessors **declare victory, healing, or provision in prayer, even before the breakthrough arrives**.

Pray as if the answer has already come. Thank God for the fulfillment of His promises, even when the evidence has yet to appear.

Identifying and Confronting Spiritual Resistance

> *"For we do not wrestle against flesh and blood, but against principalities, against powers, against the rulers of the darkness of this age." (Ephesians 6:12)*

Prophetic intercession often requires **confronting spiritual resistance**. As intercessors, we engage in spiritual warfare by **declaring God's victory over areas where the enemy has entrenched himself**. The enemy will attempt to hinder God's will, but **persistent prophetic prayer dismantles his strongholds**.

"When we speak what God has spoken, the power of darkness trembles. The gates of hell cannot stand against a believer who prays with the authority of Christ."

Lake described encounters with demonic opposition, which he overcame by **standing on the authority of Christ and declaring God's word until the resistance was broken**. Intercessors must do the same— **stand firm, declare God's word, and refuse to back down** until the enemy flees.

When you sense resistance, **persist in prophetic prayer**. Declare God's promises boldly and confront the enemy with unwavering faith.

Prophetic Prayer Changes Nations and Situations

"Ask of Me, and I will make the
nations your inheritance." (Psalm 2:8)

Prophetic intercession is not limited to personal situations—it has the power to **shape the nations**. Throughout history, God has raised up intercessors to stand in the gap and **declare His purposes over cities, governments, and generations**.

"The prayers of one Spirit-filled believer can alter the course of history. When we pray, heaven responds, and the earth must align with God's will."

Lake's ministry transformed cities in South Africa, where entire regions were impacted by the power of God. **Prayer shaped the spiritual landscape**, bringing revival and healing. Prophetic intercessors are called to do the same—**speak life over nations, declare revival, and release God's kingdom on earth**.

Pray big prayers. Don't limit your intercession to personal concerns—**declare God's will over your city, nation, and generation.**

Speak What God Speaks, and the Earth Will Shift

Prophetic intercession is **prayer that carries the power of heaven**. It is prayer that **listens to the Holy Spirit, speaks with authority, and declares God's promises into existence**. As intercessors, we do not beg—we **proclaim the will of God boldly** and refuse to back down until we see His promises fulfilled.

God's word in your mouth is as powerful as His word in His own mouth. Speak it, and the mountains will move.

The next chapter will explore **how intercession impacts the world and prepares the way for the Spirit to move in power**. But remember this: **Prophetic prayer is not passive—it is the declaration of God's will with authority and faith**. Speak what God speaks, and the earth will shift.

Chapter 9

BRINGING CHANGE THROUGH INTERCESSION

God's Response to Persistent Prayer

*I*t is the flame of prayer that ignites the outpouring of the Spirit —it is the response to hearts on fire with intercession.

Change begins in the place of prayer. Every great move of God throughout history involved **intercession**, where believers cried out to God. It is not accidental. **It comes when men and women align their hearts with God's desire to pour out His Spirit and refuse to relent until they see it happen.**

This chapter will explore the role of intercessors in **initiating change, preparing the ground for awakening, and sustaining the move of God once it begins**.

Burdened Prayer

> *"As soon as Zion travailed, she brought forth her children." (Isaiah 66:8)*

Change always starts with **a burden in the heart of the intercessor**. God places His desire for transformation within those who are willing to pray, and **this becomes a holy fire that cannot be quenched**. Intercessors feel the weight of the spiritual condition around them.

"When the burden of God rests on you, it will drive you to your knees. Prayer is no longer optional—it becomes a burning necessity."

In 1906, revival broke out at Azusa Street, but it began long before with small groups of believers **praying and weeping over their city**. They carried the burden of revival in prayer until God's Spirit moved powerfully. John G Lake was also known to **travail in prayer for days** until he saw miracles and breakthroughs. **The Spirit's burden within you is a sign that God is moving**.

Ask God for His burden. Pray for the Spirit to show you what breaks His heart and let it fuel your prayers for change.

Clearing the Way: Repentance Precedes Revival

"If My people, who are called by My name, will humble themselves and pray and seek My face and turn from their wicked ways, then I will hear from heaven." (2 Chronicles 7:14)

Before a move of God, **the ground must be cleared through repentance**. Intercessors stand in the gap, not only confessing their own sins but also **identifying with the sins of their communities and nations, crying out for cleansing and renewal**. God's move cannot take root in hardened hearts—it requires humility.

Intercession plows the hardened soil of the heart, making it ready for the rain of the Spirit. Without repentance, the seed of revival cannot grow.

In Lake's time, cities were changed because **believers repented on behalf of the people, confessing sin and crying out for God's mercy.** They recognized that personal and corporate repentance was essential. Similarly, the Welsh Revival was born as believers **wept over their sin and cried out for God to cleanse the land**.

Pray for personal and corporate repentance. Ask God to expose anything that hinders His Spirit and lead you to pray for cleansing over your life, church, and community.

Sustaining what God is doing through Watchful Prayer

"Watch and pray, lest you enter into temptation." (Mark 14:38)

God moving through prayer is one thing, **but sustaining a move or work requires continual intercession. The enemy will try to disrupt and derail the move of God**, but intercessors must remain vigilant, standing as watchmen on the walls.

During the revivals Lake was a part of, **prayer never ceased**. Believers organized 24-hour prayer watches to ensure that the flame of revival would not die out. In. these times, **the intercessor's role is to guard what God is doing**, praying for protection, purity, and continued outpouring.

Establish rhythms of continual prayer. Form prayer watches and be vigilant in intercession, especially during seasons of big moves of God.

It is Contagious: Spreading the Fire through Prayer

"I have come to bring fire on the earth, and how I wish it were already kindled!" (Luke 12:49)

A move of God is not meant to remain in one place—it is designed to **spread like wildfire**. Through prayer, intercessors can **carry the flame from one region to another**. When a move breaks out in one location, **intercessors fan the flames through prayer and declarations** until entire cities and nations are set ablaze.

Pray for it to spread. Don't limit your prayers to your own church— **declare a move of God over cities, regions, and nations**. Ask God to extend the fire wherever the Spirit leads.

Laboring in Prayer Until the Spirit Comes

Revival is the result of **persistent, Spirit-led intercession**. It requires **burdened hearts, repentance, travail, and watchful prayer** to see the outpouring of God's Spirit. But the reward is great—lives transformed, communities renewed, and nations touched by the power of God.

Revival is not a distant hope—it is the inheritance of those who will labor in prayer until heaven opens. Intercessors are the midwives of awakening.

The next chapter will explore **the role of fasting in intercession** and how it accelerates things. But remember this: **if you will pray with the fire of God in your heart, revival will come.**

Chapter 10

FASTING AND INTERCESSION— ACCELERATING

Fasting is Power in Action

*F*asting is the cutting edge of intercession. It sharpens the soul and places the spirit in perfect alignment with God's purposes. When you fast, your prayer life becomes a conduit for the power of heaven.

There are times when prayer alone isn't enough to deal with something—**it requires fasting**. Fasting is not about manipulating God; it is about **removing blockages in our own soul and releasing spiritual power**. Jesus said that certain kinds of spiritual strongholds cannot be broken without **prayer and fasting (Mark 9:29)**. Fasting accelerates God's purposes, heightens spiritual discernment, and removes obstacles that hinder the manifestation of the Spirit.

Fasting is the intercessor's secret **weapon**, a tool that silences the voice of the flesh and allows the Spirit to reign supreme. This chapter will explore how fasting and intercession work together, destroy demonic opposition, and create an atmosphere where the miraculous becomes the norm.

Fasting Aligns You with the Spirit of God

"Man shall not live by bread alone, but by every word that proceeds from the mouth of God." (Matthew 4:4)

When you fast, **you disconnect from the natural in order to connect with the spiritual**. Fasting teaches you to live not by the strength of your body, but by the life of the Spirit. **Your sensitivity to God's voice increases**, and your prayers carry more precision and power. Lake believed that **fasting clears the noise of the world** and opens the intercessor to hear the Holy Spirit with clarity.

"The man or woman who fasts becomes a sharpened instrument in the hand of God. The Spirit finds no resistance in a life emptied of self."

Lake often recounted that during seasons of fasting, **his awareness of the Spirit's presence heightened dramatically.** He would fast for days, sometimes even weeks, as he prayed for breakthroughs. **During those times, miracles flowed effortlessly**—not because of his strength but because the Spirit was fully in charge.

When you fast, **expect your spirit to become more sensitive** to the promptings of the Holy Spirit. Ask God to show you what He is doing and pray accordingly.

Fasting Breaks Spiritual Strongholds

"This kind does not go out except by | prayer and fasting." (Matthew 17:21)

Certain spiritual strongholds can only be broken through **the combination of fasting and prayer**. There are times when the enemy's grip on a situation is so entrenched that only a consecrated life—one marked by fasting—can break through. **Fasting adds force to your intercession** and confronts the powers of darkness directly.

"The kingdom of darkness trembles when a believer fasts and prays. Fasting unlocks realms of power that cannot be accessed in any other way."

When you sense persistent opposition in prayer, **consider adding fasting** to your intercession. Expect spiritual breakthroughs and bondages to be broken as you fast.

Fasting Prepares You

"Then Jesus, full of the Holy Spirit, returned from the Jordan and was led by the Spirit into the wilderness." (Luke 4:1)

After fasting for 40 days, **Jesus returned in the power of the Spirit** and began His public ministry with miracles and healing. **Fasting opens the door to supernatural manifestations**. The intercessor who fasts is preparing the way for God to release miracles, signs, and wonders. Lake believed that fasting positioned the believer to be a **conduit of the miraculous**.

When you fast, you are positioning yourself on the front lines of the miraculous. You are making room for God's Spirit to move through you with power.

In South Africa, Lake witnessed **entire regions impacted by the power of God** following seasons of fasting and prayer. People were healed, demons were cast out, and entire communities were transformed. He firmly believed that **fasting prepared the spiritual atmosphere for miracles**.

Fast when you are believing for miracles. Whether it is healing, deliverance, or revival, fasting will prepare the way for the Spirit to move.

Fasting Sustains Spiritual Breakthroughs

"Do not grow weary in well-doing, for in due season you shall reap if you do not lose heart." (Galatians 6:9)

Fasting is not just for initiating breakthroughs—it is essential for **sustaining them**. Many moves of God have begun in power only to fade because believers grew weary in prayer and fasting. **Sustained spiritual success requires continual consecration**. Fasting keeps the heart humble and dependent on God, preventing pride from creeping in.

The man who lives a fasted life is one whom the enemy cannot control. He is not swayed by the appetites of the flesh—he is ruled by the Spirit.

Commit to a fasted lifestyle, even when the breakthrough comes. Regular fasting will keep your heart humble and your spirit aligned with God.

Corporate Fasting: United Prayer for Greater Breakthroughs

"Proclaim a holy fast; call a sacred assembly." (Joel 1:14)

There is a unique power in **corporate fasting**, when believers come together to fast and pray as one. **Corporate fasting unifies the church and amplifies the power of intercession**. Lake believed that **when believers fast as a group, the Spirit of God is stirred in a profound way** that cannot be replicated by individual efforts alone.

A church that fasts together is a church that walks in power. The Spirit will move mightily where there is unity in fasting and prayer.

Lake witnessed **entire congregations fasting and praying together**, resulting in extraordinary breakthroughs. The unity of their fasting released a **powerful corporate anointing** that transformed communities. Corporate fasting creates **momentum** in the Spirit, drawing the church into deeper unity and greater effectiveness in prayer.

Organize times of corporate fasting with your church or prayer group. As you fast together, expect God to move powerfully in your midst.

Fasting Unlocks the Full Power of Intercession

Fasting is a powerful tool in the hands of the intercessor. **It sharpens the spirit, breaks strongholds, and prepares the way for the miraculous**. Through fasting, believers align themselves with God's purposes and release His power into situations that would otherwise remain unchanged. **The combination of fasting and intercession creates an unstoppable force** that the enemy cannot withstand.

The man who prays and fasts walks in power. He carries the authority of heaven and is a terror to the kingdom of darkness.

In the next chapter, we will explore **the rewards of perseverance in intercession** and how persistence unlocks the promises of God. But remember this: **If you will fast and pray, nothing shall be impossible for you.**

Chapter 11

THE REWARDS OF PERSEVERANCE IN INTERCESSION

God Rewards Those Who Do Not Quit

*P*erseverance in prayer is not a sign of defeat but of victory in the making. The intercessor who refuses to quit will see the reward of their faith. God's promises are sure, and the one who presses in will receive what has been promised.

God is a **rewarder of those who diligently seek Him** (Hebrews 11:6). The prayers of the persistent intercessor never go unanswered, even when the answer seems delayed. The greatest victories often come to those who are willing to persevere in faith, pressing in through opposition, delay, and discouragement. **Perseverance in intercession is an act of faith**—faith that believes that what God has promised will surely come to pass.

There was a moment sometime around 2012 when I felt the Spirit prompt me to begin to pray for Russel Brand to come to truly know God. He had been on an interview that happened to be on my parents TV one day when I felt this prompting. He had mentioned receiving a blessing from some nuns who had been on set. It wasn't until 2024 that he became a professing Christian. This demonstrates to me the power of persevering prayer.

This chapter will explore the **spiritual rewards that come through persevering prayer**, both in this life and in eternity. It will also discuss the reasons for delays, the importance of enduring through trials, and the power that comes to those who refuse to give up.

God's Promise to Reward Faithful Prayer

"And let us not grow weary while doing good, for in due season we shall reap if we do not lose heart."(Galatians 6:9)

God has promised that **persistent prayer will always result in a harvest**. There are no prayers that go unheard, no intercessions that go unnoticed by heaven. Sometimes the answer comes immediately, but often, **the greatest breakthroughs require time and perseverance**. The intercessor who persists in prayer will reap a reward in due season—**if they do not grow weary and give up**.

Every seed sown in prayer will produce a harvest. It may not be visible today, but the fruit of your intercession is guaranteed if you remain steadfast.

Stay consistent in your prayer life. Even when you don't see the immediate result, know that God is faithful to reward those who seek Him diligently.

Understanding Delays in Prayer

"The vision is yet for an appointed time... though it tarries, wait for it, because it will surely come."(Habakkuk 2:3)

Delays in answered prayer are often misunderstood as **denial**, but in reality, delays are part of God's process. **There is an appointed time for every answer to manifest**. In some cases, the delay serves to strengthen our faith and refine our hearts, preparing us for the answer that is to come. In other cases, **spiritual opposition may delay the answer**, but it will come to those who press in. **Delay is not defeat—delay is often a preparation for greater victory**.

The intercessor who understands that delays are not denials will persevere in faith, knowing that God's timing is always perfect.

Daniel fasted and prayed for 21 days before receiving his answer (Daniel 10). **The angel who brought his answer was delayed by spiritual warfare in the heavens**, but the answer came because Daniel did not give up. **His perseverance broke through the resistance.** In the same way, there are times when spiritual forces resist the answers to our prayers, but as we persist, **the opposition is broken and God's answer is released**.

When you face delays in prayer, **stand firm**. Remind yourself of God's promises and trust that the delay is part of His divine process.

Perseverance Builds Character and Power

"But let patience have its perfect work, that you may be perfect and complete, lacking nothing." (James 1:4)

Perseverance in prayer does more than bring the answer—it **transforms the intercessor**. Through persevering prayer, God is at work shaping the character of His people, teaching them to rely on His strength, and developing a deeper intimacy with Him. **The process of waiting strengthens our faith, builds patience, and deepens our dependence on God's power**. The greater the trial, the greater the growth.

The intercessor who endures is being made into a vessel of greater power. The longer the wait, the deeper the work, and the more profound the reward.

Lake often spoke of the **spiritual power that comes through enduring hardship**. His own ministry was marked by perseverance through incredible difficulties—sickness, persecution, and financial lack. But through every trial, God was refining him and preparing him for greater works of power. The same is true for every believer—**perseverance in prayer increases spiritual authority**.

Embrace the process of waiting and refinement. Know that as you persevere in prayer, God is working in you, strengthening your spirit and building greater power for the breakthroughs ahead.

The Power of Persistence in Spiritual Warfare

"Resist the devil, and he will flee from you." (James 4:7)

Persistence in prayer is often necessary in **spiritual warfare**. The enemy will attempt to resist God's plans, especially when they are close to being fulfilled. **It is in the moment of greatest resistance that the intercessor must press in even harder, knowing that the victory is near.** Spiritual warfare requires not only bold authority but also the **endurance to keep praying until the enemy is defeated**.

"The enemy can resist for a season, but he cannot withstand the intercessor who refuses to quit. Satan's power is no match for persistent prayer."

Frequently engaging in **spiritual warfare** means confronting sickness, demonic oppression, and strongholds in cities. Know that the enemy's resistance is strongest just before the breakthrough, but also know that **persistence in prayer always wears the enemy down**. Victory belongs to those who persist.

In moments of spiritual warfare, **do not retreat**. Keep pressing in with declarations of God's word, binding the enemy, and praying for the manifestation of God's will.

The Eternal Rewards of Perseverance

"Blessed is the man who endures temptation; for when he has been approved, he will receive the crown of life."
(James 1:12)

There are not only rewards in this life for persevering in prayer—**there are eternal rewards**. God honors those who labor in prayer, and **their efforts will bear fruit not only on earth but in heaven**. The intercessor who persists in prayer will be rewarded for every prayer, every tear, and every moment of endurance. **Nothing is wasted.**

"Every hour of intercession, every sacrifice, is counted in heaven. The one who labors in prayer will receive a crown of glory in eternity."

It is important to understand that the rewards of persistent prayer extend beyond the earthly ministry. I believed that **every victory won in prayer has eternal significance** and that God will reward those who give themselves to the work of intercession. Passion for prayer is driven not only by a desire to see earthly results but also by **a deep conviction that every prayer moves heaven and shapes eternity**.

Remember that your prayers have eternal value. What you labor for in the Spirit today will be rewarded both now and in the life to come. Let this truth fuel your perseverance.

Keep Pressing, The Reward is Coming

Perseverance in prayer is the key to seeing God's promises fulfilled. **Though the journey may be long, the reward is sure**. The intercessor who refuses to quit will see the breakthrough, for God is faithful to His word. Keep praying, **keep pressing, and do not give up**. God is working, and the reward is on its way.

The intercessor who endures to the end will see the hand of God move mightily. The reward is not for the one who starts but for the one who finishes.

In the next chapter, we will explore **how intercessors leave a legacy of faith** that impacts generations. But remember this: **if you keep praying, you will see the reward of your faith**. God is faithful to fulfill every promise.

Chapter 12

LEAVING A LEGACY OF INTERCESSION

A Life of Prayer Shapes Generations

*T*he work of intercession doesn't end when the prayer meeting is over. Every prayer you pray plants seeds that grow into a harvest, not just for today, but for generations to come.

The life of an intercessor is not confined to their own lifetime. **Every prayer you pray, every battle you win in the Spirit, and every victory you see manifest creates a ripple effect that touches future generations**. Intercessors are the ones who prepare the ground for future outpourings of God's Spirit, who break strongholds over nations, and who establish spiritual foundations that others will build upon.

In this chapter, we will explore how **intercession leaves a legacy of faith, revival, and transformation**. The work of intercessors doesn't stop with them—it continues through those who come after them, affecting their families, churches, communities, and even entire nations.

The Power of Generational Blessing Through Prayer

"The generation of the upright will be blessed." (Psalm 112:2)

Intercession releases generational blessings. Your prayers for your family, children, and descendants don't just affect the present—they create a spiritual inheritance that **will shape their future**. Intercessors stand in the gap for their families, breaking curses, securing promises, and establishing legacies of faith. **Your prayers today are the foundation of their victories tomorrow.**

When you pray for your family, you are not only shaping their present, but securing their future. Your prayers lay a foundation of blessing that will last for generations.

John G Lake often spoke of how his mother's fervent prayers established a legacy of faith in his life. **He was the product of a praying family, and that legacy of prayer continued through him and his ministry.** Generational blessings are the fruit of persistent intercession.

Pray intentionally for your family and future generations. Declare God's promises over your children, grandchildren, and beyond, believing that your prayers will carry a legacy of blessing.

Building Spiritual Foundations for Future Generations

"They will rebuild the ancient ruins and restore the places long devastated." (Isaiah 61:4)

The intercessor's prayers are like **building blocks** that lay a foundation for future generations. Your prayers establish things that others will walk in, **clear obstacles that would have blocked future progress**, and open doors that others will walk through. **You are rebuilding spiritual walls that have been broken down, preparing the way for those who will come after you.**

Every prayer is a brick in the spiritual foundation of your family, community, and nation. You are building something that will outlast you.

Ministry doesn't just affect those in this generation—it lays the groundwork for revivals and movements of God that come after you. **Intercessors today are still walking in the spiritual foundations that**

others laid. Your prayers will establish a foundation that future generations will stand upon.

Pray with a long-term perspective. Understand that every prayer you pray is building something that will impact generations to come. **See your intercession as foundational work** that others will build upon.

Breaking Curses and Establishing Freedom for Future Generations

"Christ redeemed us from the curse of the law by becoming a curse for us." (Galatians 3:13)

Intercessors have the authority to **break generational curses** and release blessings that will impact future generations. Many families, communities, and even nations labor under spiritual oppression and curses that have been passed down through generations. **Through intercession, you have the power to break those strongholds and release freedom** for your descendants.

The intercessor's prayers are like an axe laid to the root of generational curses. What bound your family in the past will no longer bind them in the future.

Christian leaders throughout history have often spoke of **families and individuals bound by sickness, poverty, or oppression**, only to be set free by prayer. There are many stories of **entire family lines changed** as intercessors prayed and broke the chains of generational bondage. The same is true today—**your prayers can change the future of your family line** by breaking what has held them captive.

Pray to break generational curses over your family and community. Use the authority of Christ to bind what has held them in bondage and release God's freedom over future generations.

Leaving a Legacy of Faith in Your Community and Nation

"I sought for a man among them who would make a wall, and stand in the gap before Me on behalf of the land." (Ezekiel 22:30)

Intercessors don't just leave a legacy for their family—they leave a legacy for **their community and nation**. Every prayer for revival, every act of intercession for righteousness, every cry for justice and mercy creates **a spiritual shift** that affects the land. **Intercessors are the ones who shape the spiritual landscape of nations, calling forth God's purposes and restraining evil.**

The intercessor stands between heaven and earth, releasing the will of God over nations. The prayers you pray for your country today will impact generations to come.

John G Lake's ministry in South Africa not only transformed individual lives—it **shifted the spiritual atmosphere of entire regions**. His prayers and ministry created a legacy of revival and transformation that **continued long after he had left**. Similarly, the prayers of intercessors today can shape **the destiny of their nations,** calling forth righteousness, justice, and revival.

Pray for your city, region, and nation with the understanding that your prayers are shaping their future. Your intercession can leave a lasting legacy of transformation.

Leaving a Legacy of Intercession in the Church

"The effectual fervent prayer of a righteous man avails much." (James 5:16)

Intercessors leave a legacy not only in their family and nation but also in **the church**. A praying church is one that walks in power, and intercessors are the ones who **carry the spiritual weight** of the church's growth, protection, and advancement. **The intercessor lays the groundwork for future revivals, movements, and ministries** within the church. **Your prayers sustain the church's mission** and leave a legacy for future generations of believers.

Your prayers create the spiritual climate for revival, growth, and power.

Churches have often been built and sustained through the prayers of intercessors who labored in prayer day and night. **The spiritual power of the church was directly tied to the fervency of its intercessors.** Intercessors today leave a similar legacy—**creating the spiritual conditions for future generations to experience revival, power, and growth.**

Pray for your church and its future generations. Ask God to raise up more intercessors, and pray for the church to grow in power, influence, and revival in the years to come.

Your Prayers Will Outlast Your Time Here

The life of an intercessor is not limited to the present moment. **Your prayers will continue to bear fruit long after you are gone.** Every act of intercession, every prayer for revival, and every declaration of God's will leaves a legacy that future generations will benefit from. **The work of prayer transcends time and impacts eternity.**

The intercessor leaves behind a trail of miracles, breakthroughs, and transformations that will touch lives for generations to come. Your prayers are an inheritance of power that will never fade.

As we conclude this journey, remember that **the life of intercession is a life of eternal impact.** You are not only shaping the present—you are shaping the future. Continue to press in, knowing that your prayers are leaving a legacy of faith, revival, and transformation for those who will come after you.

Chapter 13

WALKING IN THE FULL AUTHORITY OF YOUR CALLING AS AN INTERCESSOR

A Call to Step into Your God-Given Authority

*T*he intercessor is not an ordinary person—they are a conduit of heaven, a vessel of divine power, and a warrior in the kingdom of God. To stand in the gap is to take your place in the eternal purposes of God, releasing His will upon the earth with power and authority.

This chapter is a **call to action**. You have journeyed through the principles of communion, authority, persistence, fasting, and prophetic prayer. **Now is the time to step fully into the mantle of intercession**. God is calling for a new generation of intercessors—those who will stand in the gap, who will pray until heaven moves, and who will live lives completely surrendered to the Spirit.

In this chapter, we will explore the final steps of **embracing your identity as an intercessor**, walking daily in the authority God has given you, and committing to a life of prayer that will impact the world around you. **The world needs intercessors more than ever**, and God is calling you to be a part of His plan to release revival and transformation on the earth.

Recognizing the Weight of Your Calling

*"I sought for a man among them who
would make a wall, and stand in the gap
before Me on behalf of the land." (Ezekiel 22:30)*

Intercession is not just a spiritual activity—it is **a high calling from God**. You have been chosen to **stand in the gap**, to represent the will of God on earth, and to bring His kingdom to every situation. This is not a light task—it carries the weight of eternal significance. **God is seeking those who will take this calling seriously, who will devote their lives to prayer and intercession**.

To be an intercessor is to carry the heart of God, to feel His burden for the lost, and to release His power into the world. It is the highest honor and the greatest responsibility.

Intercession **is the backbone of every move of God**. Often there are hidden, unseen warriors of the kingdom—those who prayed in secret but changed nations through their prayers. **You are called to be one of those warriors**, standing in the gap, unseen by men but fully known by God.

Accept the full weight of your calling. Understand that your role as an intercessor has eternal implications and that your prayers shape the destiny of nations and individuals alike.

Walking Daily in Spiritual Authority

*"Behold, I give you the authority to trample on serpents
and scorpions, and over all the power of the enemy, and
nothing shall by any means hurt you." (Luke 10:19)*

To walk in your calling as an intercessor, you must walk in **the authority that God has given you**. You are not a passive participant in spiritual matters—you are an ambassador of Christ, carrying the authority of His kingdom. **This authority is not theoretical—it is real and available to you every day**. As an intercessor, you have the power to **bind and loose,**

to declare and to command, because you are operating under the authority of heaven.

The intercessor must walk in the confidence of their authority. You are not standing before God as a beggar—you are seated with Christ, speaking from a place of victory.

Paul the apostles ministry was marked by a bold confidence in the authority of Christ. He never prayed from a place of doubt but **from a place of victory, knowing that the authority of heaven was backing every word**. Intercessors today must walk in that same boldness, **knowing that every prayer spoken in faith moves mountains**.

Begin to pray from your position in Christ. Speak with the authority He has given you, knowing that your prayers carry the power to shift atmospheres and release the purposes of God.

Living a Life Fully Surrendered to the Spirit

"For as many as are led by the Spirit of God, these are the sons of God." (Romans 8:14)

To be an effective intercessor, you must live a life that is **fully surrendered to the Holy Spirit**. The Spirit is the source of all power, discernment, and revelation in prayer. **Your life must be one of continual dependence on the Spirit**, allowing Him to guide your prayers, direct your actions, and shape your character. Intercession flows from a life that is yielded to the Spirit, where the desires of the flesh are put aside, and the will of God is your only pursuit.

The man or woman who is filled with the Spirit is unstoppable in prayer. They pray with power because they are not praying their own words—they are praying the very will of God.

Some of my biggest mentors and mothers and fathers have been those whose lives were marked by an extraordinary sensitivity to the Holy Spirit. People who will often pause in the middle of a meeting to listen for the Spirit's direction, refusing to act until they are sure of God's leading. **This**

same sensitivity is required of intercessors—to live in step with the Spirit and allow Him to direct every prayer.

Cultivate a life of listening and surrender. Before you pray, pause and listen for the Spirit's leading. Allow Him to direct your prayers and fill your heart with His desires.

Rise Up, Intercessor—The World Needs Your Prayers

The world is in desperate need of intercessors—**those who will stand in the gap, carry the burdens of heaven, and release God's will upon the earth**. The time for complacency is over. **Now is the time to rise up and take your place** as a warrior in the kingdom, as a vessel through whom God's power flows.

The call to intercession is a call to change the world.

Chapter 14

THE POWER OF A PURE HEART – BUILDING STRONG CHARACTER IN THE LIFE OF AN INTERCESSOR

Character is the Foundation of Powerful Prayer

*T*he intercessor's authority in prayer flows directly from their relationship with God. A heart that is pure before the Lord is a vessel through which the Spirit can flow freely. Without purity, even the most fervent prayers lose their power.

True spiritual authority doesn't just come from knowing techniques or principles—it comes from **living a life of holiness and purity before God**. The intercessor's effectiveness is directly tied to their relationship with the Father, and **the condition of the heart** determines how freely God's power can flow through them.

This is a subject that my great uncle Charles Sharpe often preached on. As a young man it sometimes felt like he overemphasized the importance of character. The inspirational life that he lived was one that should make you take note of the emphasis he placed on character to sustain the move of God.

One of my other biggest heroes in the faith was someone who put a large emphasis on purity of heart. This person was someone who was known to walk in the miraculous and signs in wonders more so than any one else

I have heard of. He was actually one of the big inspirations for me to go to ministry school in the first place. Unfortunately he allowed bitterness to take root in his heart. Bitterness can be a tricky thing. It's like quicksand in the spirit because the more you address it, the bigger it gets. At least when you address it in an earthly way.

Bitterness is really just long term unforgiveness that disguises itself as something else. It will seem like concern or justice or maybe even compassion in some instances. Sometimes it will come across as a little "harmless" resentment. It's easy for a seasoned intercessor to identify unforgiveness, so unforgiveness likes to masquerade through bitterness as something more noble.

It was only after I allowed the seeds of bitterness in my life for some years that I learned this the hard way. Allowing room in my life for someone who had walked away from their calling and was partnering with bitterness cost me dearly. In many ways it slowly seeped into my life and lead me away from God, then away from church, then eventually it had a significant role in the end of my marriage.

Thank God for the community of believers of fathers, mothers, and mentors in my life. Thank God for repentance and restoration that God has made always available for us. Bitterness is not something to be taken lightly and is something that should be weeded out of the intercessors life as soon as possible.

I talked with a good friend in ministry from my time at school in California and he had gone through a rough journey around the same time frame as me. He pointed out how it was so easy to step into the momentum of that move of God but we lacked the character to sustain it for ourselves. I think at those young ages its so easy to show up passionate and think it will be enough. However, there was a lot of wisdom in my uncle Charlie's emphasis on time tested strength of character and integrity. As a believer and as an intercessor you can step into a move of God and drink from that well and gain from that momentum. At the end of the day, however, there is no substitute for having the strength of character as an individual to move in what the Spirit of God is doing.

In this chapter, we will explore the importance of keeping your heart pure, building strong character, and living a life of integrity. Without these things, even the most passionate prayers are hindered. But when your heart is aligned with God's holiness, your intercession becomes a powerful force for change.

The Connection Between Purity and Power

"Blessed are the pure in heart, for
they shall see God." (Matthew 5:8)

Purity of heart is the foundation of powerful intercession. Those who keep their hearts pure are able to see and discern the will of God clearly, allowing them to pray with precision and authority. Sin, unforgiveness, bitterness, and pride can block the flow of the Holy Spirit, weakening the effectiveness of your prayers. **A heart that is pure before the Lord creates an open channel for His power to flow through**.

Powerful prayer begins with a pure heart. A heart free from sin is a vessel for the fullness of God's Spirit.

Charlie Sharpe's ministry was marked by **a deep commitment to personal holiness**. He understood that **the power of God flowed through purity**, and he often taught that sin in the life of a believer could quench the flow of the Holy Spirit. Charlie urged believers to **confess sin regularly,** live with a clean conscience, and walk in holiness so that nothing would hinder their prayers.

Examine your heart daily. Confess sin, release any unforgiveness, and ask the Holy Spirit to cleanse you from anything that could block your prayers.

Guarding Your Heart Against Bitterness and Offense

"Above all else, guard your heart, for everything
you do flows from it." (Proverbs 4:23)

Bitterness, offense, and unforgiveness are some of the greatest obstacles to powerful intercession. When we hold onto offense, we close off our hearts to the fullness of God's love and power. **The intercessor must guard their heart fiercely**, choosing to forgive quickly and keep their spirit free from resentment. The enemy loves to use offense to block the flow of prayer, but **a heart that forgives freely remains open to God**.

The intercessor's heart must be a place where offense has no foothold. The enemy will try to plant seeds of bitterness, but you must uproot them immediately.

Charlie often dealt with people who had suffered deep offenses and carried unforgiveness in their hearts. He would explain that **holding onto offense blocked the very power of God they were seeking**. He emphasized the importance of forgiveness, not just for the sake of peace, but because **unforgiveness hinders prayer**.

Choose to forgive quickly. Refuse to let offense take root in your heart, knowing that **bitterness blocks the power of your prayers**.

Integrity: The Hidden Strength of an Intercessor

"The integrity of the upright will guide them, but the perversity of the unfaithful will destroy them."(Proverbs 11:3)

Integrity is the backbone of the intercessor's life. It means being the same person in private as you are in public, living with honesty, faithfulness, and transparency. **God honors those who walk in integrity**, and your prayers gain strength when your character is aligned with His holiness. The intercessor who walks in integrity becomes a trusted vessel for God's purposes, able to stand in the gap with confidence.

The intercessor's life is not only measured by their prayers but by their character. Integrity is the hidden strength that gives power to your prayers.

Charlie's life and ministry were known for their deep commitment to integrity. He believed that **powerful prayer could only come from a life**

that was aligned with the righteousness of God. Intercessors who walk in integrity are trustworthy before God, and their prayers are potent because they come from a place of truth and righteousness.

Live with integrity in every area of your life. Guard your heart against compromise, knowing that God blesses those who walk in righteousness.

Keeping a Humble and Teachable Spirit

"God opposes the proud but gives
grace to the humble." (James 4:6)

Humility is essential in the life of an intercessor. **Pride blocks the manifestation of grace**, while humility opens the door to greater authority in prayer. The intercessor who remains humble before God will continually grow in wisdom, discernment, and spiritual authority. **Pride assumes that we know what is best, but humility keeps us in a posture of dependence on the Holy Spirit**.

The greatest intercessors are those who have learned to bow low before God, knowing that all power comes from Him.

Charlie Sharpe often warned against **spiritual pride** in those who experienced great power in prayer. He emphasized that the believer must **always remain humble and teachable**, understanding that their authority comes not from themselves but from Christ. **Humility keeps the heart soft and open to God's correction and leading**.

Remain teachable. Ask the Holy Spirit to correct any areas of pride in your life, and continually acknowledge that your authority and power come from God alone.

Living in Constant Dependence on God's Grace

"My grace is sufficient for you, for My power is
made perfect in weakness." (2 Corinthians 12:9)

The intercessor's life must be lived in **constant dependence on God's grace**. You will never be able to pray effectively in your own strength—it is only by the power of the Holy Spirit that you can fulfill your calling. **God's grace sustains you in times of trial, weakness, and fatigue**. When your strength runs out, His grace fills the gap, empowering you to continue.

It is not your strength that will see you through—it is God's grace. The intercessor who learns to rely on grace will find themselves empowered in every season.

Charlie understood that **human strength is insufficient** for the spiritual work of intercession. He often spoke of times when **God's grace carried him** through difficult seasons. He taught that **grace is the source of power** for every intercessor, sustaining them in times of weakness.

Lean on God's grace in your intercession. When you feel weak or weary, remember that **His power is made perfect in your weakness**.

Character and Purity Sustain the Life of an Intercessor

The power of an intercessor's life is not found in outward actions alone—it is rooted in the purity of the heart and the strength of their character. A heart that is aligned with God's holiness, free from offense, and marked by integrity and humility will be a powerful vessel for the purposes of heaven. **Your prayers are only as strong as the condition of your heart**. As you walk in purity and character, God will entrust you with greater authority, and your prayers will carry the power to change lives, families, and nations.

If you will keep your heart pure, God will entrust you with His power. Your life of prayer will move mountains and release heaven's purposes on earth.

As we close this chapter, remember that a **life of powerful intercession is not sustained by methods or techniques—it is sustained by purity, character, and a life fully surrendered to God**. Walk in holiness, live with integrity, and keep your heart open to the Spirit's leading, and you will become a vessel of great power in the kingdom of God.

For more information on the inspirational life of Charles N Sharpe I would highly recommend his book Turning Points. The ministry he planted still exists and thrives in Bethel Missouri, helping people get their lives moving in a positive direction and walk with God.

Chapter 15

WILLIAM BRANHAM – THE PROPHETIC AND HEALING POWER OF GOD IN ACTION

A Man of Uncommon Anointing

*T*he gifts and callings of God are irrevocable. When a man surrenders to God's purpose, His power flows through them in ways that can shake the world. William Branham was such a man—a humble servant through whom God demonstrated the prophetic and healing power in an extraordinary way.

William Branham was an American evangelist and prominent figure in the mid-20th-century healing revival. His ministry was marked by **unparalleled prophetic accuracy, stunning healings, and miracles** that confirmed the power of God at work. **Branham's life is a testimony to what God can do through a person who is yielded to the Holy Spirit, walking in deep communion with God and moving in faith and obedience**.

This chapter will examine the life of William Branham and explore the **prophetic and healing dimensions of his ministry**, the impact of his work on the broader Christian landscape, and how **intercession and prophetic insight** work hand in hand to release God's power today.

The Early Life and Call of William Branham

"Before I formed you in the womb I knew you,
before you were born I set you apart; I appointed
you as a prophet to the nations." (Jeremiah 1:5)

William Branham's life began with a sense of divine calling. **From an early age, he experienced supernatural encounters** that would mark him for ministry. At the age of seven, he had a vision in which he heard a voice saying, *"Never drink, smoke, or defile your body in any way. There will be a work for you to do when you get older."* This encounter, followed by others, set the stage for a life of **miracles, visions, and divine encounters** that shaped his prophetic and healing ministry.

"Branham's early encounters with God were not random—they were a divine preparation for a prophetic ministry that would touch nations."

Just like many, **Branham was called from an early age**, with a specific purpose to bring God's word to the people. His childhood was marked by hardship, but through it all, **God was preparing him** for a ministry that would later change the course of countless lives.

Recognize that God's call often comes with divine preparation. Allow your personal experiences, even the difficult ones, to shape you for the ministry God has for you.

The Healing and Prophetic Anointing on William Branham

"And these signs will follow those who believe:
In My name they will cast out demons; they will
speak with new tongues; they will lay hands on
the sick, and they will recover." (Mark 16:17-18)

Branham's ministry became known for its incredible demonstrations of **healing power and prophetic precision. He moved with a deep sensitivity to the Holy Spirit, often receiving visions and words of knowledge about**

individuals before he even met them. As a result, thousands came to his meetings to receive healing and deliverance. His reputation grew as he ministered with an anointing that could only come from God.

One of the most remarkable aspects of his ministry was **the prophetic accuracy** with which he would describe a person's illness, life situation, or specific details of their past before praying for their healing. **Branham did not see healing as separate from the prophetic**—he believed that the word of God revealed through prophecy often prepared the way for the manifestation of healing.

"Branham's ministry was a demonstration of the Spirit and power. Through prophetic words and healing prayers, God's kingdom broke into the lives of people, bringing healing, restoration, and deliverance."

In one notable instance, **Branham prophesied in great detail about a woman's life and condition before laying hands on her for healing**. As he spoke, the woman broke down in tears, recognizing that only God could have revealed those details. **As Branham prayed, the woman was healed instantly**. Such events were commonplace in his meetings, where the prophetic flowed hand in hand with healing.

Embrace the prophetic dimension of healing. When praying for healing, ask the Holy Spirit to reveal specific insights that will unlock the door to faith and healing.

The Role of Intercession in William Branham's Ministry

"The effective, fervent prayer of a righteous man avails much." (James 5:16)

Intercession played a key role in William Branham's life and ministry. **He often spent long hours in prayer before his meetings, seeking God's direction and power.** He knew that **the prophetic and healing anointing flowed more freely when the atmosphere had been saturated with prayer**. Branham believed that **healing was not only a gift of the Spirit** but something that could be accessed through persistent prayer and faith.

Branham understood that miracles are often birthed in prayer. The intercessor stands in the gap, creating the spiritual environment for healing to manifest.

Branham's ministry was often supported by **teams of intercessors** who prayed throughout his meetings. These intercessors created an atmosphere where **the presence of God was tangibly felt** and where miracles flowed effortlessly. Branham recognized that without intercessory prayer, the power of God might not break through as powerfully as it could.

Incorporate intercession as a foundation for healing ministry. Whether you are praying for one person or a group, understand that **intercessory prayer prepares the way for the Spirit's power** to flow in healing and prophecy.

How God Uses Prophecy to Build Faith for Healing

"Pursue love, and desire spiritual gifts, but especially that you may prophesy." (1 Corinthians 14:1)

One of Branham's most profound insights was **how prophecy builds faith for healing**. When a person heard specific details about their life revealed through prophecy, it sparked faith within them that **God saw their need and was ready to heal them**. Prophecy, in this way, was often the **catalyst for healing,** as it stirred faith in the hearts of those who received it.

"When God speaks prophetically, He reveals His will and builds faith. That faith then becomes the platform upon which healing is released."

In one instance, **Branham prophesied over a man who was paralyzed, revealing details about the man's past that no one could have known**. As Branham spoke, **the man's faith was ignited, and he believed that healing was possible**. When Branham laid hands on him, the man immediately began to walk—his faith had been unlocked through the prophetic word.

Seek the prophetic when praying for healing. Ask God to speak words of knowledge or prophecy that will build the faith of those in need.

The Continuing Legacy of William Branham's Ministry

"You shall receive power when the Holy Spirit has come upon you; and you shall be witnesses to Me in Jerusalem, and in all Judea and Samaria, and to the end of the earth." (Acts 1:8)

Though William Branham passed away in 1965, his ministry left a profound impact on the church and the world. **His emphasis on the supernatural power of God, the prophetic, and healing has continued to influence generations of ministers and believers**. Many modern healing evangelists and prophetic ministers trace their roots back to the revivals and healing meetings led by Branham. His ministry is a reminder that **the gifts of the Spirit are alive and active today** and that God still uses ordinary people to do extraordinary things.

Branham's legacy lives on in the many who have been inspired to pursue the gifts of the Spirit. His life stands as a testimony to what God can do through a surrendered heart.

The ripple effect of Branham's ministry can be seen in the **Charismatic and Pentecostal** movements that have swept through the church in the decades since his passing. Many of the healing ministries that emerged in the latter half of the 20th century were directly influenced by Branham's teachings and example. **His life and ministry serve as an enduring inspiration for those who seek to walk in the fullness of God's power.**

Honor the legacy of those who have walked before us by continuing to press into the prophetic and healing ministries. **God is still moving today,** and He desires to work through every believer who is willing to step out in faith.

Chapter 16

JOHN WESLEY – REVIVAL THROUGH PRAYER AND HOLINESS

A Man Consumed by the Fire of God

*G*ive me one hundred preachers who fear nothing but sin, and desire nothing but God, and I care not a straw whether they be clergymen or laymen; such alone will shake the gates of hell and set up the kingdom of heaven upon earth.

—John Wesley

John Wesley was one of the greatest revivalists in Christian history, a man whose dedication to **prayer, holiness, and the power of the Holy Spirit** helped to ignite spiritual fires that spread across England and beyond. His heart burned with a desire to see God revive **His people** and bring the transforming power of the gospel to every corner of the nation. As the founder of the **Methodist movement**, Wesley's disciplined life of prayer, his preaching, and his passion for the poor and disenfranchised became the foundation of a spiritual revival that still resonates today.

This chapter will explore **Wesley's deep commitment to prayer and intercession**, his pursuit of holiness, and how his life of devotion and spiritual discipline **sparked revival** that transformed not only individual lives but entire communities. We will look at how God used Wesley's life as an example of **what can happen when a man or woman is fully surrendered to God's will** and dedicated to persistent, faithful prayer.

John Wesley's Early Life and Conversion

"I will give you shepherds after my own heart, who will feed you with knowledge and understanding."(Jeremiah 3:15)

John Wesley's early life was shaped by his **family's deep Christian faith**, especially his mother, Susanna Wesley, whose discipline and teaching influenced his spiritual development. Educated at **Oxford University**, Wesley, along with his brother Charles, formed the "Holy Club," a group dedicated to **prayer, Bible study, fasting, and acts of charity**. This early stage of his life laid the groundwork for the discipline and holiness that would mark his future ministry.

However, despite his religious zeal, Wesley's **heart was not yet fully converted**. It wasn't until 1738, after a difficult missionary journey to America and feeling his personal inadequacy, that Wesley experienced his famous **"Aldersgate" conversion**. In his own words, *"I felt my heart strangely warmed. I felt I did trust in Christ, Christ alone, for salvation."* This **transformational encounter** with the grace of God became the catalyst for the revival that would follow.

Wesley's conversion sparked a fire that would later ignite revival. **Though disciplined in prayer and good works, it was not until Wesley experienced the personal revelation of God's** grace that his ministry took on supernatural effectiveness. His life reminds us that **prayer and intercession must be grounded in a living relationship with God, empowered by the Holy Spirit.**

Pursue a living relationship with God through prayer. Discipline is important, but it is the transforming power of grace and the Holy Spirit that brings life to intercession.

The Birth of the Methodist Movement: Revival through Holiness

"But just as he who called you is holy, so be holy in all you do; for it is written: 'Be holy, because I am holy.'" (1 Peter 1:15-16)

John Wesley's life and ministry were deeply marked by his pursuit of **holiness** and his belief that **personal and communal revival** comes through sanctification and devotion to God. **The Methodist movement**, which Wesley founded, was not simply about theology—it was about a **methodical approach to spiritual** growth and discipline, rooted in prayer, Scripture, and service to others.

Wesley believed that **revival could not come apart from holiness**. He taught that believers were called to a life of **"Christian perfection"**, not in the sense of flawlessness but in having a heart wholly surrendered to God, fully dedicated to His will. For Wesley, **holiness and revival were inseparable**, and he saw personal holiness as the fuel for the broader societal transformation that occurred during his ministry.

The revival that swept through England during Wesley's time was not born in church programs or grand sermons but in the lives of men and women consecrated to God in prayer and holy living.

One of Wesley's famous sayings was, *"The world is my parish."* This was his expression of the **radical reach of the gospel**, but also of the **methodical movement of holiness** that transformed individuals and communities. As Wesley traveled on horseback across England, preaching to tens of thousands, **his emphasis on prayer, holiness, and small groups (class meetings)** created an environment where **revival spread organically** through transformed lives.

Embrace a life of holiness. Revival begins in the heart, with a commitment to live a life fully surrendered to God. As you pursue holiness through prayer and obedience, you create the conditions for revival to flourish in and around you.

Wesley's Discipline of Prayer and Fasting: Fueling the Revival Fire

"Devote yourselves to prayer, being watchful and thankful." (Colossians 4:2)

John Wesley's ministry was not a result of chance or mere human effort—it was **undergirded by a life of deep discipline in prayer and fasting**. Wesley believed that **intercession and personal prayer** were the primary means through which God's Spirit moved in revival. He often woke up at 4 a.m. to pray and fasted two days a week, setting an example for those who followed him.

Wesley also organized **prayer meetings and "watch nights"**, where believers would gather to pray late into the night, seeking God's face for personal renewal and for the nation. These gatherings were critical in maintaining the fire of revival that was sweeping across England, as **they created an atmosphere of expectancy and hunger for God's presence**.

Prayer was the engine that drove Wesley's revival. Without prayer, there was no power, no movement of the Spirit. But where there was fervent, faithful prayer, there was an outpouring of God's Spirit.

Wesley's ministry of prayer was marked by **extraordinary discipline**, but it was also filled with fervor and expectancy. **His belief in the power of collective and individual prayer** laid the foundation for the **Methodist movement's spread across England and later to America**. These prayers not only led to conversions but also to **healings, deliverances, and societal transformation**.

Commit to a disciplined prayer life. Revival is fueled by consistent, intentional prayer. Set aside time each day for intercession, and seek God with a heart of expectancy, knowing that He is eager to respond to the prayers of His people.

Wesley's Commitment to Social Justice: The Fruit of Revival

"Is not this the kind of fasting I have chosen: to loose the chains of injustice and untie the cords of the yoke, to set the oppressed free and break every yoke?" (Isaiah 58:6)

For John Wesley, **revival was not merely a spiritual awakening—it was a call to action**. He believed that a **true move of God led to social transformation**, particularly in how people cared for the poor, the oppressed, and the marginalized. Wesley's ministry was marked by his tireless work on behalf of those who were enslaved by poverty, addiction, and injustice.

Wesley's **sermons and writings on social justice focused on the practical application of Christian faith**. He championed the abolition of slavery, the education of children, and the alleviation of poverty. He also established medical clinics, schools, and funds to care for the poor, believing that **revival must bear the fruit of justice and compassion**. For Wesley, **a church alive in the Spirit would naturally overflow into works of mercy and social justice**.

True revival touches both the soul and society. Wesley's life was a testimony that revival must not only change hearts but also transform how we live and love our neighbors.

During the height of his ministry, **Wesley famously wrote and preached against the evils of slavery**, long before it became a popular cause. His voice in this matter, as well as his advocacy for prison reform and his care for the impoverished, showed that **true revival is accompanied by the pursuit of justice and mercy** in the world.

Let your prayers for revival extend to societal transformation. Ask God to show you how revival in your heart and community can bring about justice, compassion, and mercy for those who are marginalized.

Chapter 17

BILLY GRAHAM – A VOICE FOR EVANGELISM AND GLOBAL REVIVAL

Praying for God to Do It Again

L *ord, do it again! And would You do it again through me?*
      The year was 1946, and a young **Billy Graham** was visiting
England with a group of fellow ministers. As part of their trip, they
toured historic Christian sites, including **John Wesley's home**, a sacred
space for anyone familiar with the great revivals of the past. In Wesley's
bedroom, the group was shown the two worn-out patches on the floor beside
Wesley's bed—places where Wesley had spent countless hours in fervent
prayer, asking God to bring revival to England and beyond.

As the group prepared to leave the house, they realized that **Graham
was missing**. The guide returned to Wesley's bedroom to find Graham
kneeling in the very same spot where Wesley had prayed, his knees
pressed into the worn-out patches. Graham was praying, **"Lord, do it again!
And would You do it again through me?"** He was asking God to move, just
as He had in Wesley's time, and to use him as a vessel.

This prayer became the heartbeat of **Billy Graham's ministry**—a
passionate plea for God to move in his generation with the same power that
had marked the revivals of the past. And indeed, God answered that prayer.

Through his evangelistic crusades, Graham would go on to preach the gospel to millions of people across the world, becoming one of the most influential Christian leaders of the 20th century.

The Early Life and Conversion of Billy Graham

"For I am not ashamed of the gospel, because it is the power of God that brings salvation to everyone who believes." (Romans 1:16)

Born in 1918 on a dairy farm in North Carolina, **Billy Graham** was raised in a devout Christian family. His early years were shaped by the rhythms of rural life and the influence of **Bible-believing parents**. However, Graham's personal encounter with God came at the age of 16, when he attended a revival meeting led by the traveling evangelist **Mordecai Ham**. It was at that meeting that Graham felt a deep conviction of sin and responded to the altar call, committing his life to Christ.

This moment of salvation ignited in Graham a passion for evangelism and a desire to see others come to faith in Christ. From that point forward, Graham dedicated his life to preaching the gospel, starting as a student at **Florida Bible Institute** and later at **Wheaton College**, where he further developed his understanding of Scripture and evangelistic ministry.

Billy Graham's conversion was not just the beginning of his personal faith—it was the moment that set in motion a life dedicated to bringing the message of salvation to millions.

Graham's early years were marked by a hunger to know God and a boldness to share the gospel with others. He often preached to small gatherings in rural churches, never imagining that one day he would stand before millions in arenas and stadiums around the world. **His life demonstrates how God can take the humble beginnings of a young convert and turn them into a global movement for the kingdom.**

Never underestimate the power of personal conversion. When you commit your life to God and His purposes, He can use you in ways far beyond what you imagine. Start where you are, and let God lead you step by step into His plan for your life.

The Birth of a Global Evangelistic Ministry

"Go into all the world and preach the
gospel to all creation." (Mark 16:15)

By the 1940s, **Billy Graham** had already gained a reputation as a gifted evangelist. But it was his participation in **Youth for Christ** rallies that catapulted him into the national spotlight. The young, dynamic preacher had a unique ability to communicate the gospel in a way that resonated with the masses. His passion for souls, combined with his clear and compelling presentation of the gospel, drew crowds wherever he went.

In 1949, Graham held a tent revival in **Los Angeles**, which became the turning point for his ministry. Originally scheduled for three weeks, the revival extended to eight weeks, drawing more than 350,000 people. During this time, **newspapers began to cover the meetings**, and prominent figures such as Hollywood celebrities and politicians attended. The revival put **Billy Graham** on the map, and his ministry exploded from there.

Graham's heart for evangelism led him to organize **large-scale crusades** that would eventually take him around the world. From the United States to Europe, Africa, Asia, and beyond, Graham's message of salvation through Jesus Christ reached millions. Over the course of his life, it is estimated that **Billy Graham preached to over 215 million people** in live audiences, with countless more reached through radio, television, and later, the internet.

Graham's life was a testimony to the power of obedience to the Great Commission. He answered the call to go into all the world and preach the gospel, and God used him to lead millions to salvation.

In one of his most famous crusades, **Graham preached to over 1.1 million people in Seoul, South Korea, in 1973**, with tens of thousands responding to the altar call. This was a defining moment for global evangelism, as it showed that the hunger for the gospel was not confined to the West but was a universal need.

Be willing to step out in faith and share the gospel, whether to one person or to many. God honors the faithful proclamation of His Word, and you never know how many lives may be transformed through your obedience.

The Power of Prayer in Billy Graham's Ministry

"Devote yourselves to prayer, being watchful and thankful." (Colossians 4:2)

Behind every successful evangelistic crusade and every soul won to Christ was a foundation of **prayer**. Graham understood that **prayer was the engine of revival**, and he relied heavily on prayer to sustain his ministry. Before each crusade, Graham and his team would spend time in deep intercession, asking God to move in the hearts of those who would attend.

In addition to personal prayer, Graham mobilized **large networks of intercessors** in each city where his crusades were held. These prayer warriors would begin praying weeks, sometimes months, before the events, covering every detail in prayer—from the logistics of the crusade to the spiritual readiness of the people. **Graham believed that prayer softened hearts and prepared the ground for the seeds of the gospel to take root.**

"Billy Graham knew that without prayer, even the most eloquent sermon would fall on deaf ears. It was prayer that prepared the soil of the heart, allowing the gospel to take root and bear fruit."

In one instance, **Graham recounted how the success of a crusade in London in 1954** was directly tied to the **intercession of thousands of believers** who had been praying for revival in the city. The crusade, held in Harringay Arena, lasted for three months, and **over 1.75 million people attended**, with many committing their lives to Christ. Graham often attributed the success of this and other crusades to the power of prayer.

Commit your evangelistic efforts to prayer. Whether you're sharing the gospel with a friend or leading a larger outreach, make prayer the foundation of everything you do, trusting that God will move in response to the prayers of His people.

Integrity and Humility:
The Hallmarks of Billy Graham's Life

"Whoever exalts himself will be humbled, and whoever humbles himself will be exalted." (Matthew 23:12)

One of the defining characteristics of **Billy Graham's ministry** was his commitment to **integrity** and **humility**. Despite his global fame and influence, Graham remained grounded in his mission to preach the gospel, refusing to let success inflate his ego. He surrounded himself with a team of trusted advisors who helped him stay accountable in his personal and public life.

In 1948, Graham and his team created the **"Modesto Manifesto,"** a code of conduct that outlined their commitment to financial transparency, sexual purity, and accountability. This manifesto helped Graham avoid the scandals that often plagued other high-profile leaders, allowing him to maintain a ministry marked by moral integrity and trustworthiness.

"Billy Graham's legacy is not only in the millions of souls won to Christ but also in the example he set for integrity and humility in ministry. His life is a reminder that true greatness in the kingdom of God comes from serving with a pure heart."

Throughout his life, **Graham turned down lucrative offers** that could have made him wealthy, choosing instead to live modestly and devote himself to his calling. His humility and refusal to take advantage of his fame were key factors in the longevity and **fruitfulness of his ministry**. He consistently directed attention away from himself and toward **Jesus Christ**, refusing to let personal accolades overshadow the gospel message. Graham's ministry remained free from scandal, and his reputation for integrity allowed him to gain the trust of world leaders and everyday people alike.

Pursue integrity and humility in all areas of life and ministry. True spiritual authority comes from walking in integrity before God and others. Commit to transparency and accountability, knowing that these qualities will guard your ministry and strengthen your witness.

Billy Graham's Global Impact and Legacy

"You will receive power when the Holy Spirit comes on you; and you will be my witnesses in Jerusalem, and in all Judea and Samaria, and to the ends of the earth." (Acts 1:8)

Billy Graham's influence extended far beyond the borders of the United States. His global ministry took him to over 185 countries, where he preached the gospel to millions, including people in communist countries, war-torn regions, and nations closed off to traditional Christian missionary work. Graham was often welcomed by world leaders and government officials because of his reputation for integrity, and he took every opportunity to preach Christ wherever he went.

Graham's message was simple yet profound: **salvation through Jesus Christ**. His ability to communicate the gospel in a way that transcended cultural, political, and denominational boundaries made him a bridge-builder in the global Christian community. His meetings were often ecumenical, drawing people from different church traditions into a shared encounter with the message of salvation.

Billy Graham's legacy continues through the work of the **Billy Graham Evangelistic Association (BGEA)**, which remains committed to spreading the gospel worldwide through crusades, media outreach, and humanitarian work. His influence is also seen in the lives of countless pastors, evangelists, and Christian leaders who were inspired by his ministry and have gone on to impact the world for Christ.

Billy Graham's life was a fulfillment of the Great Commission. Through his ministry, millions heard the gospel, and his legacy continues to inspire the church to take the message of Christ to the ends of the earth.

In 1982, Graham preached to over 100,000 people in **Moscow, Soviet Union**, an event that was unheard of during the Cold War. Graham's message of reconciliation and hope transcended the ideological barriers of the time, and his ability to bring the gospel into such contexts showed the **global reach of God's word.**

Expand your vision for how God can use you globally. Whether through direct outreach, prayer, or support of missions, every believer has a role in fulfilling the Great Commission. Be open to how God might use you to spread His message to the ends of the earth.

Conclusion: A Life of Obedience and Revival

Billy Graham's life is a testimony to what God can do through a person who is fully committed to Him. **From his humble beginnings on a North Carolina farm to his global evangelistic ministry, Graham's passion for revival and his dedication to prayer shaped his entire life**. His commitment to preaching the simple, uncompromised message of the gospel led to millions of lives being transformed by the power of Jesus Christ.

"The secret of Billy Graham's success was not in his eloquence or fame but in his deep reliance on God through prayer, humility, and obedience. He simply followed the call to preach Christ and trusted God to bring the harvest."

As we conclude this chapter, let Billy Graham's life inspire you to embrace your own calling to share the gospel, to **pray fervently for revival**, and to live with integrity and humility. Just as Graham knelt in John Wesley's room and prayed, **"Lord, do it again,"** we too can ask God to move in our generation with the same power and conviction, believing that He is ready to answer.

Ask God to "do it again" in your life. Just as Graham prayed for revival to come to his generation, seek God for a fresh outpouring of His Spirit in your life, your community, and your world. Be bold in sharing the gospel and faithful in prayer, trusting that God can use you to bring others to Christ.

Chapter 18

JOHN G. LAKE – A LIFE OF FAITH, HEALING, AND INTERCESSION

A Life of Radical Faith and Divine Healing

*F*or as many as are led by the Spirit of God, they are the sons of God.

—John G. Lake

John G. Lake was a man whose ministry was marked by extraordinary demonstrations of **divine healing, miracles, and deep faith in the power of God**. Known as one of the great pioneers of the **Pentecostal movement**, Lake's life was dedicated to teaching and demonstrating that **the power of the Holy Spirit** that was present in the early church is still available to believers today. His healing rooms in Spokane, Washington, were so effective that the city was declared "the healthiest city in America" during his ministry there.

Lake believed that intercession and the ministry of **healing** were interconnected, and that the power of God flowed through a life committed to both. This chapter will explore Lake's early life, his experiences in South Africa as a missionary, and his later ministry in the United States. Above all, it will show how **John G. Lake's faith in God's healing power** continues to inspire believers today to walk in authority and deep intimacy with God.

The Early Life and Call of John G. Lake

"The Spirit of the Lord is upon me, because He has anointed me to preach the gospel to the poor; He has sent me to heal the brokenhearted, to proclaim liberty to the captives and recovery of sight to the blind." (Luke 4:18)

John G. Lake was born in **Ontario, Canada** in 1870 and later moved to the United States. His early life was marked by suffering and loss. Several of his family members, including his mother and siblings, suffered from serious illnesses. Lake watched helplessly as they battled disease, and this led him to question the power of God in relation to healing. However, his perspective radically changed when his family began to experience miraculous healings through prayer, including the dramatic healing of his wife, Jennie, who was healed from a terminal illness.

This encounter with God's healing power marked a turning point in Lake's life. He began to study the Scriptures with new eyes, believing that **healing was part of the atonement of Jesus Christ** and available to all believers. His personal experiences with healing stirred within him a deep faith in God's ability to heal today, just as He had in the days of Jesus and the apostles.

John G. Lake's early experiences with sickness and healing fueled his passion for the ministry of divine healing. He became convinced that healing was not an optional gift but a central part of the gospel.

After seeing his wife miraculously healed, **Lake's hunger for more of God's power intensified**. He devoured the Scriptures, focusing on passages where Jesus and the apostles healed the sick. Lake became convinced that the same power that healed in biblical times was still accessible to believers who would walk in faith. **This revelation transformed his life and ministry**, launching him into the supernatural dimensions of healing and deliverance.

Study the Scriptures with a heart open to God's healing power. Just as John G. Lake's understanding of healing came through a deep study of

God's Word, commit yourself to learning and believing in the promises of God for healing.

The South Africa Mission: Bringing Healing to the Nations

"And they went out and preached everywhere, the Lord working with them and confirming the word through the accompanying signs." (Mark 16:20)

In 1908, **John G. Lake and his family felt called to become missionaries** in South Africa. With only a few dollars in his pocket and no guaranteed support, Lake embarked on a journey of faith, believing that God would provide for every need. His time in South Africa became one of the most fruitful seasons of his ministry, marked by **miraculous healings, revival, and the establishment of over 500 churches**.

Lake's ministry in South Africa was known for its powerful healing services, where **thousands were healed of all kinds of diseases**. His preaching was accompanied by signs and wonders, and it wasn't uncommon for entire communities to experience **revival and transformation** as people were healed, delivered, and brought to faith in Christ. **Divine healing became the hallmark of his ministry**, and people from all over the country flocked to hear him preach and receive prayer for healing.

John G. Lake believed that God's healing power was not just for individuals but for nations. His ministry in South Africa demonstrated that when the gospel is preached with faith and power, entire regions can be transformed by the Spirit of God.

During his time in South Africa, Lake recounted numerous instances of healing. One of the most famous accounts was during a **bubonic plague outbreak**, where Lake laid hands on the sick, and many were instantly healed. In one instance, doctors watched in awe as **Lake touched the foam from a victim's mouth**, and it dissolved under the microscope, demonstrating the power of God over disease. **This act of faith left a lasting impression**, and many more were healed as a result.

Step out in faith when God calls you. John G. Lake didn't wait for perfect conditions before answering God's call. He moved in obedience, trusting that God would meet him with power. If God has called you to minister to others, trust Him to provide both the resources and the power to fulfill your calling.

Spokane Healing Rooms:
The Power of Intercession and Healing

"The effective, fervent prayer of a
righteous man avails much." (James 5:16)

After returning to the United States, John G. Lake felt led to open **healing rooms** in Spokane, Washington. These rooms were places where people could come and receive prayer for healing. **Lake and his team of trained prayer ministers** interceded for the sick, laying hands on them and declaring God's healing power over their lives. The results were astonishing—**over 100,000 documented healings occurred in five years**, and Spokane was declared "the healthiest city in America" during his ministry.

Lake believed that healing wasn't limited to special moments but could be part of the everyday life of believers. He trained others in **healing ministry**, teaching them how to lay hands on the sick with confidence in God's power.

John G. Lake knew that intercession was the key to unlocking heaven's healing power. Through fervent, persistent prayer, Lake and his team saw thousands of lives transformed, and the supernatural became the norm.

Lake's healing rooms were a **testament to the power of persistent prayer**. One account tells of a young boy who was paralyzed from birth. After receiving continuous prayer for healing in the healing rooms, the boy stood up and walked, shocking both his family and the community. **This kind of miraculous healing was common** in Lake's ministry, and it all flowed from a foundation of intercession and unwavering faith.

Build a foundation of intercessory prayer. Whether you're praying for healing or for revival, commit to persistent, fervent intercession. God responds to the prayers of His people, and the results can be extraordinary when faith and prayer work together.

The Supernatural Power of Faith: Walking in Authority over Sickness

"He Himself bore our sins in His body on the tree,
that we might die to sin and live to righteousness.
By His wounds you have been healed." (1 Peter 2:24)

John G. Lake taught that **every believer has access to the supernatural power of God** and can walk in authority over sickness and disease through the finished work of Jesus Christ. He believed that healing wasn't just for a select few—it was part of the **inheritance of every Christian**. Lake's faith was rooted in the conviction that **Jesus' atoning work on the cross included healing**, and he lived out that conviction with boldness and authority.

Lake emphasized that believers could access this power through faith. He often said that **faith is the currency of heaven**, and those who truly believe will see the power of God manifested in their lives. Lake's boldness in praying for the sick was a direct result of his unshakeable belief in God's ability and willingness to heal.

"Healing is not an occasional act of mercy; it is a daily manifestation of God's power available to those who believe."

Lake's boldness in the face of sickness was legendary. One story recounts how he was called to pray for a man on his deathbed. As Lake entered the room, he laid hands on the man and prayed with the authority of someone who believed **heaven had already secured the victory**. The man, who had been bedridden for months, immediately sat up and began to regain his strength. This was just one of countless examples in which **Lake's faith in the healing power of God** produced immediate, miraculous results.

John G. Lake never prayed timid or uncertain prayers. He knew that when he prayed in faith, he was exercising the authority that Jesus had given to every believer. **His life was a demonstration of what it means to pray with boldness and expect results**. He believed that healing was part of the atonement of Christ and that believers could walk in the authority of that truth.

Pray with the boldness of faith. When you pray for healing, do so with the full confidence that God desires to heal and that Jesus' work on the cross has already secured that healing. **Bold, faith-filled prayers open the door for the miraculous to occur**.

The Legacy of John G. Lake: A Life of Miracles and Faith

"These signs will follow those who believe: In My name they will cast out demons; they will speak with new tongues; they will take up serpents; and if they drink anything deadly, it will by no means hurt them; they will lay hands on the sick, and they will recover." (Mark 16:17-18)

John G. Lake's legacy is one of deep faith, extraordinary miracles, and a life fully yielded to the power of the Holy Spirit. His **healing ministry** inspired generations of believers to pursue God's supernatural power, and his teaching on faith and intercession continues to shape ministries worldwide. His healing rooms, which saw over 100,000 healings in just five years, became a model for other ministries to follow, and his unwavering belief that **God still heals today** has been passed down to modern healing ministries and movements.

Even after his death in 1935, **John G. Lake's influence** continues. His writings, sermons, and the testimonies from his ministry have inspired countless believers to walk in faith and to boldly believe in the miraculous. Lake's life is a reminder that **the supernatural power of God is available to all believers today** and that healing is part of the inheritance of the saints.

John G. Lake's life and ministry showed the church that the miracles of the New Testament were not confined to the apostles—they are meant to be part of the everyday life of believers who walk in faith.

Lake's teaching on **divine healing and faith** has influenced modern healing ministries, including organizations that continue to operate healing rooms modeled after Lake's original ministry in Spokane. His legacy has been instrumental in shaping **the Pentecostal and Charismatic movements**, where faith in God's healing power is still a central part of ministry.

Carry the legacy forward. John G. Lake believed that every believer could walk in the power of God. Take hold of that same faith and apply it in your own life, trusting that God's healing power and miraculous works are still available today.

Embracing the Fullness of God's Healing Power

John G. Lake's life serves as a powerful reminder of the **potential of a believer fully surrendered to the Holy Spirit**. His ministry was marked by radical faith, persistent prayer, and the demonstration of God's power through healing. **He challenged the church to believe for the impossible**, knowing that God's power is not limited by time or circumstances.

As we conclude this chapter, let Lake's life inspire you to **pursue the fullness of God's healing power**. Whether you are praying for personal healing, interceding for others, or seeking a deeper understanding of how God works through faith, know that the same Spirit that empowered John G. Lake is alive and available to you today. **Healing is part of your inheritance as a believer, and faith unlocks the door to the supernatural.**

Embrace the call to walk in the Spirit. Just as John G. Lake lived in the reality of God's healing power, step out in faith and begin to heal with the confidence that God is still healing today. Let Lake's life be an inspiration to pursue the miraculous, trusting in the power of God's Spirit at work in and through you.

Chapter 19

SMITH WIGGLESWORTH – THE MINISTER OF FAITH AND MIRACLES

A Life of Radical Faith and Power

If the Spirit does not move me, I move the Spirit.

—Smith Wigglesworth

Smith Wigglesworth was a man of **unshakable faith** who walked in the miraculous power of God like few others in modern history. Born in 1859 in England, Wigglesworth came from humble beginnings, working as a plumber before experiencing a radical encounter with the power of God. His ministry became famous for the miraculous healings that took place wherever he preached, and he had a reputation for being a man who believed God's Word without question.

Wigglesworth's faith in God's ability to heal, raise the dead, and transform lives made him one of the most influential healing evangelists of the early 20th century. He traveled the world, praying for the sick, preaching with boldness, and challenging the church to believe that the same power that raised Jesus from the dead was available to them. His life is a testament to what is possible when a believer fully trusts in the promises of God and moves in the power of the Holy Spirit.

Smith Wigglesworth's Early Life and Call to Ministry

"And my God will meet all your needs according to the riches of his glory in Christ Jesus." (Philippians 4:19)

Smith Wigglesworth was born into a poor family in Yorkshire, England, and began working at a young age. His early years were marked by **poverty and hardship**, and he had very little formal education. However, from a young age, Wigglesworth had a hunger for God and experienced moments of deep spiritual encounters. He became a Christian as a child, but it wasn't until he married his wife, Polly, a devout Christian, that his faith began to grow in depth and power.

Polly, who was a powerful preacher in her own right, initially led their family in ministry, while Wigglesworth supported her from the background. However, after an intense **baptism in the Holy Spirit**, Wigglesworth's life and ministry were transformed. **He began to see miracles, healings, and even resurrections** as he boldly stepped into his calling as an evangelist. Wigglesworth's life of **radical obedience** to God quickly became known for supernatural power.

"Smith Wigglesworth was an ordinary man who became extraordinary because of his unshakable belief in God's promises. His radical faith in the power of the Holy Spirit transformed his life and ministry."

Wigglesworth often spoke of his early reluctance to preach, letting Polly lead their ministry. But after **his baptism in the Holy Spirit**, everything changed. He began to preach with power and boldness, and soon **miracles began to follow him everywhere he went**. One of his early accounts involved a man who was miraculously healed of a terminal illness after Wigglesworth prayed for him. **This marked the beginning of a ministry filled with supernatural signs and wonders**.

Embrace the power of the Holy Spirit. Just as Smith Wigglesworth's life was transformed after receiving the baptism of the Holy Spirit, seek God's Spirit in your own life, trusting that the same power is available to you.

Uncompromising Faith: Moving in the Power of God

"Jesus said to him, 'If you can believe, all things are possible to him who believes.'" (Mark 9:23)

Smith Wigglesworth was known for his **uncompromising, bold faith**. He took God's Word literally and believed that whatever the Bible said, God could and would do. He was not one to doubt or hesitate when it came to praying for the sick or believing for the impossible. His famous saying, *"Only believe,"* became the hallmark of his ministry, and it was through this simple yet profound faith that **thousands were healed and delivered**.

Wigglesworth did not allow circumstances or appearances to shake his faith. Whether it was terminal illness, physical disability, or even death, **he believed that God's power could overcome any obstacle**. His faith was often tested in situations where others might have given up, but Wigglesworth's unwavering trust in God's ability to do the impossible kept him moving forward.

Faith is an act. It is believing God's Word above all else and taking action in response to that belief. Wigglesworth understood that the key to moving in the power of God was simple, childlike faith.

One of the most famous stories of **Smith Wigglesworth's radical faith** was when he prayed for a man who had been dead for several hours. Wigglesworth boldly lifted the man from his deathbed, stood him against a wall, and commanded him to walk in Jesus' name. After several attempts, **the man miraculously came back to life**. This kind of boldness was typical of Wigglesworth's ministry—he refused to accept defeat and trusted in the supernatural power of God to perform miracles.

Exercise bold faith in your prayers. Smith Wigglesworth believed that when God promises something in His Word, we can take Him at His word and pray with boldness. When you pray for healing, provision, or deliverance, trust that God will move in response to your faith.

Healing and Miracles:
Demonstrations of the Spirit's Power

"They will lay hands on the sick,
and they will recover." (Mark 16:18)

Smith Wigglesworth's ministry was marked by **remarkable healing miracles**. Whether it was people suffering from cancer, paralysis, blindness, or other chronic conditions, Wigglesworth prayed for them with the expectation that they would be healed. His belief in the healing power of Jesus was unshakable, and he refused to let doubt or fear enter his mind when praying for the sick.

He would often pray for people in unconventional ways, sometimes commanding sickness to leave with authority or even physically moving someone's body in faith that they would be healed. His methods may have seemed strange to some, but **the results spoke for themselves**. Thousands of people testified of being healed under his ministry, and Wigglesworth consistently gave the glory to God.

"Wigglesworth did not simply pray for healing—he expected healing. His prayers were filled with the confidence that Jesus' power was present and available to heal all who came to Him in faith."

One account tells of **Wigglesworth praying for a woman with cancer**, who had been given no hope by doctors. Instead of praying a gentle prayer, **he rebuked the cancer**, commanding it to leave in the name of Jesus. The woman was instantly healed and went on to live a healthy life. **Wigglesworth's belief in the authority of the believer to cast out sickness** was a key part of his ministry, and many experienced healing as a result of his bold prayers.

Pray with the authority of a believer. Wigglesworth believed that believers have the authority to speak to sickness and command healing in Jesus' name. When you pray for healing, do so with the confidence that you are exercising the authority that Christ has given you.

The Importance of Holiness and Consecration

"But just as he who called you is holy,
so be holy in all you do." (1 Peter 1:15)

Wigglesworth was not only known for his faith and healing ministry but also for his **commitment to holiness and consecration**. He believed that living a life set apart for God was essential for walking in the power of the Holy Spirit. Wigglesworth famously said, *"I cannot understand God by feelings; I understand God by what the Word says about Him. I cannot build on the sands of time and circumstances; I build on the solid rock of God's Word."*

He lived a life of prayer and deep devotion to God, avoiding anything that he believed would distract him from his relationship with the Lord. He would spend hours in prayer and fasting, believing that a **life of holiness allowed the power of God to flow freely through him**.

Wigglesworth knew that power in ministry was directly connected to a life of holiness. He understood that a consecrated life was a vessel through which the Holy Spirit could move unhindered.

Wigglesworth was known to **avoid secular distractions** and lived a life of simplicity, focused on prayer and the study of God's Word. He often urged other believers to live in a way that honored God, avoiding anything that would grieve the Holy Spirit. He believed that **holiness was not an option for those who desired to walk in the miraculous**—it was a requirement.

Chapter 20

JOHN ALEXANDER DOWIE – THE PATH TO DIVINE HEALING

Introduction: The Emergence of a Healer

D *ivine healing is the removal by the power of God of the disease that has come upon the body. Healing is for all.*
—John Alexander Dowie

John Alexander Dowie was a pioneering figure in the faith healing movement of the late 19th century. Before he founded the city of **Zion, Illinois**, his life was marked by a deep desire to see God's power manifest through **divine healing**. While Dowie later became known for his controversial teachings and establishment of a theocratic community, his early years were characterized by fervent belief in the healing power of God and a mission to restore biblical practices of healing to the church.

Born in Scotland and later ministering in **Australia and the United States**, Dowie's early ministry was shaped by the challenges of sickness and suffering in his own life and in the communities he served. His journey into **faith healing** began with a radical encounter with God during a time of widespread illness, and this event set the course for his entire ministry. This chapter will explore Dowie's early life, his call to ministry, and the experiences that led him to embrace and promote **divine healing** as a central tenet of the Christian faith.

The Early Life of John Alexander Dowie: Shaped by Sickness and Faith

"He sent out His word and healed them, and delivered them from their destruction." (Psalm 107:20)

John Alexander Dowie was born in 1847 in Edinburgh, Scotland, into a devout Christian family. His father, a tailor, and his mother, a deeply spiritual woman, raised him with a strong sense of Christian morality and faith. However, **Dowie's early life was marked by illness**, both his own and that of others around him. He frequently experienced sickness, and these encounters with suffering instilled in him a profound desire to understand God's power over disease.

At the age of 13, Dowie's family immigrated to **Australia**, where he would eventually begin his ministry. After a brief period in secular employment, Dowie felt called to enter the ministry, and he pursued **theological education** to prepare himself for a life of service to God. Despite the traditional theological training he received, **Dowie was deeply dissatisfied with the church's failure to address physical healing** as part of the gospel. This dissatisfaction would later push him toward embracing the **biblical promises of healing** for the sick.

Dowie's early life, marked by sickness and a deep dissatisfaction with traditional Christian responses to disease, became the foundation for his pursuit of divine healing. He believed that the gospel must include the healing of the body as well as the soul.

In his early ministry, Dowie often reflected on his personal experiences with sickness. He would later describe how, during his youth, he had often felt powerless in the face of illness. This personal history with disease **fueled his determination to discover what the Bible had to say about healing**, and it laid the foundation for his radical belief in **divine healing**.

Look for God's purpose in your challenges. Just as Dowie's early struggles with sickness became the catalyst for his healing ministry, your personal challenges may be shaping you for a future work of God. Seek to understand how God is preparing you through the difficulties you face.

A Radical Encounter with Divine Healing in Australia

"Jesus Christ is the same yesterday, today, and forever." (Hebrews 13:8)

Dowie's shift from traditional ministry to a focus on **divine healing** began during a devastating plague that swept through Sydney, Australia, in 1876. At the time, Dowie was pastoring a **Congregational church**, and the plague was ravaging his congregation. He found himself performing **multiple funerals a day**, and the suffering of his people weighed heavily on his heart. As he prayed and searched the Scriptures, Dowie experienced a **personal revelation of God's healing power**.

One day, after visiting a dying parishioner, Dowie returned home in anguish, crying out to God for understanding. In that moment, he was struck by the words of **Acts 10:38**, which spoke of Jesus healing "all who were oppressed by the devil." Dowie became convinced that **sickness was an oppression of the devil** and that healing was part of the atonement of Christ. This revelation changed the course of his ministry. He began to pray for the sick with newfound faith and authority, and **miracles began to occur**.

Dowie's revelation of divine healing was not born out of intellectual study alone—it was birthed in the trenches of suffering, as he sought God for answers in the midst of a deadly plague.

Shortly after this revelation, **Dowie prayed for a young girl in his congregation** who was on the verge of death due to the plague. He rebuked the spirit of infirmity in the name of Jesus, and the girl was instantly healed. Word of this miracle spread, and soon, **Dowie's ministry became known**

for miraculous healings, as more and more people came to him seeking divine intervention.

Seek God for revelation in times of crisis. Dowie's revelation about healing came during a time of great suffering. When faced with challenges, draw close to God in prayer and the study of His Word, trusting that He will reveal His purposes in the midst of adversity.

Controversy and Expansion: Dowie's Healing Ministry Gains Momentum

"And these signs will follow those who believe:
In My name they will cast out demons; they
will speak with new tongues; they will lay hands
on the sick, and they will recover." (Mark 16:17-18)

As news of the miraculous healings in Dowie's ministry spread, controversy began to surround him. Many in the traditional church viewed his emphasis on healing as unorthodox or even dangerous. Dowie's bold claims about divine healing challenged the medical community, and he often found himself at odds with both **church leaders and physicians**, particularly because he taught that faith in God's healing power should replace reliance on medicine. This stance led to **arrests and public outcry**, but it also drew increasing numbers of people to his ministry.

Despite the controversy, Dowie's healing ministry expanded rapidly. He began holding **healing meetings** throughout Australia, where hundreds of people experienced miraculous healings. Dowie's message was clear: **Jesus Christ had not changed**, and the same healing power that had been present in the early church was available to believers today. His uncompromising belief in the promises of Scripture drew many to his cause, and his following grew both in Australia and internationally.

Dowie's refusal to compromise his beliefs, even in the face of public opposition, made him both a controversial figure and a powerful voice for the reality of divine healing in his generation.

One of the most notable moments in Dowie's early ministry came when **he was arrested for practicing medicine without a license**. Dowie had prayed for the sick, and several prominent healings had occurred, drawing attention from the authorities. Despite the charges, Dowie continued to preach and pray for **healing, arguing that healing was part of the gospel and not medical practice**. His boldness in the face of legal and public pressure only fueled his ministry further.

Stand firm in your convictions. Like Dowie, you may face opposition when you step out in faith to believe God for the impossible. Stay rooted in Scripture and trust that God will defend His Word, even when others challenge you.

Bringing the Message of Healing to the United States

"I am the Lord, who heals you." (Exodus 15:26)

By the late 1880s, **Dowie's ministry had expanded beyond Australia**, and he felt called to bring his message of divine healing to the United States. Dowie believed that America was ripe for revival and that the message of healing was central to that revival. He began holding **healing crusades** in major U.S. cities, including San Francisco, St. Louis, and Chicago, where he preached the gospel and prayed for the sick with great success.

It was during his time in **Chicago** that Dowie's ministry began to take on a new level of influence. His healing meetings in Chicago drew thousands of people, and **miraculous healings** continued to occur regularly. In 1893, during the **World's Columbian Exposition**, Dowie set up a healing tent just outside the fairgrounds, where he prayed for the sick and preached to the multitudes. This event marked a turning point in his ministry, as **Dowie became a national figure** in the faith healing movement.

Dowie's move to the United States was strategic, as he sought to bring the message of healing to a country that was experiencing both spiritual hunger and skepticism. His success in Chicago established him as a leading figure in the faith healing movement, despite the controversies that surrounded him.

Dowie's ministry in the United States, particularly in Chicago, gained significant attention. His boldness in proclaiming that **divine healing was a part of the gospel** attracted both followers and critics. Many people from across the nation traveled to hear Dowie preach and to receive prayer for healing, while others challenged his teachings and methods. Yet, Dowie remained steadfast in his belief that **healing was available to all** who believed in the power of Jesus Christ.

During his time in Chicago, Dowie established **healing homes** where the sick could come and receive prayer. These homes became centers of ministry, and countless testimonies of healing emerged from these places. His healing ministry not only transformed lives but also sparked debates within the broader church and medical communities about the nature of faith, healing, and medicine.

Expand your reach when God opens doors. Just as Dowie brought the message of healing from Australia to the United States, trust that God may open new opportunities for you to share His message or ministry in new places. When He leads, follow with boldness and faith.

Dowie's Early Ministry –
The Foundation for Healing and Faith

John Alexander Dowie's journey before the founding of Zion, Illinois, was one marked by **radical faith, opposition, and miraculous healing**. His early years in Australia, and later in the United States, set the foundation for a ministry that would challenge traditional Christian views on healing and establish him as one of the most controversial yet influential leaders in the **divine healing movement**.

Dowie's relentless belief in the power of God to heal, coupled with his boldness in the face of opposition, made him a **pioneering figure**. His willingness to challenge both the church and the medical establishment of his time left a lasting impact on the Christian world, and his legacy continues to be felt today in the ongoing **healing and charismatic movements**.

As we close this chapter, let Dowie's story inspire you to **pursue God's promises** with unwavering faith, even in the face of challenges. His life reminds us that **God's power to heal** is still at work today, and those who are willing to step out in faith can experience the miraculous.

Be bold in your faith, even in the face of opposition. Like Dowie, don't let criticism or challenges deter you from pursuing God's calling on your life. Stand firm in His promises and trust that He will work miracles through your obedience and faith.

Chapter 21

JESUS, THE ULTIMATE INTERCESSOR – MIRACLES BORN FROM PRAYER

Jesus, Our Eternal Intercessor

"Therefore He is also able to save to the uttermost those who come to God through Him, since He always lives to make intercession for them." —Hebrews 7:25

Jesus Christ is not only the Son of God and our Savior, but He is also the **ultimate intercessor**, continually standing in the gap for humanity. The Bible tells us that even now, **Jesus intercedes for us at the right hand of the Father** (Romans 8:34). Throughout His earthly ministry, we see how Jesus' heart for intercession was expressed both in His **prayer life** and in the **miracles He performed**. Every healing, deliverance, and supernatural act flowed out of His deep communion with the Father and His compassion for people.

In this chapter, we will explore **Jesus' role as an intercessor** and the ways in which His miracles were directly connected to His prayers and His deep concern for those in need. From healing the sick to raising the dead, **Jesus' life was a demonstration of God's power working through intercession**. His example challenges us to see intercession not just as prayer, but as the means through which **God's kingdom is manifested on earth**.

Jesus' Prayer Life: The Foundation of His Intercession

"Very early in the morning, while it was still dark, Jesus got up, left the house and went off to a solitary place, where He prayed." (Mark 1:35)

Jesus' ministry was grounded in **constant prayer**. Throughout the Gospels, we see Jesus withdrawing to pray, often before significant events or miracles. His time alone with the Father was the foundation of His **intercessory ministry**. In these moments of solitude, Jesus interceded for the people He would minister to, aligning His will with the Father's and preparing for the work ahead.

Jesus' prayer life is a model for us of **what it means to live a life of intercession**. Before He healed the sick or performed miracles, He prayed. His miracles flowed out of His **intimate relationship with the Father**, and His intercession on behalf of others was the natural outflow of that relationship.

Jesus' prayers were not simply requests for power—they were moments of deep communion with the Father, out of which flowed the miracles that transformed lives.

In the Garden of Gethsemane, we see one of the most powerful examples of Jesus' intercession. As He faced the cross, **He prayed earnestly for His disciples and for all who would believe** in Him (John 17). Even in His greatest moment of personal anguish, Jesus was focused on interceding for others, demonstrating the **selflessness of His intercessory role.**

Make prayer the foundation of your ministry and life. Like Jesus, prioritize communion with the Father. Intercession flows from intimacy with God, and miracles are the result of aligning our will with His through prayer.

Healing the Sick: Intercession in Action

"And great multitudes followed Him,
and He healed them all." (Matthew 12:15)

Jesus' ministry was filled with **miraculous healings**, and every healing was an act of intercession. He stood in the gap between the **sickness of humanity** and the healing power of God. Jesus not only prayed for people, but He also brought about their healing through **words of authority**, acts of compassion, and the laying on of hands. His miracles were not isolated events—they were the visible **manifestation of His intercession** for those who were suffering.

Jesus' healing ministry shows us that **intercession is more than words**—it is a movement of the Spirit that brings about tangible change. Whether He was healing a leper (Matthew 8:2-3), restoring sight to the blind (John 9), or curing the woman with the issue of blood (Mark 5:25-34), Jesus was interceding for them, standing in the gap between their sickness and God's desire to heal.

"When Jesus healed the sick, He was interceding on their behalf, bringing them into alignment with the Father's will for their healing and wholeness."

One of the most powerful examples of Jesus' healing as an act of intercession is the story of the **paralyzed man** brought to Jesus by his friends (Mark 2:1-12). The man's friends interceded for him, bringing him to Jesus, and **Jesus responded not only to their faith but also to the man's need**. He first forgave the man's sins, an act of spiritual intercession, and then healed his body, showing the full scope of Jesus' intercessory work—healing both body and soul.

Pray for the sick with boldness. Just as Jesus interceded for the sick and brought healing, you too can pray with confidence that God desires to heal. As you intercede for others, expect God's power to be manifested through your prayers.

Casting Out Demons: Deliverance through Intercession

"When Jesus saw that a crowd was running to the scene, He rebuked the impure spirit. 'You deaf and mute spirit,' He said, 'I command you, come out of him and never enter him again.'" (Mark 9:25)

Throughout His ministry, **Jesus cast out demons**, delivering people from spiritual oppression. Every act of deliverance was a form of **intercession**, where Jesus stood between the demonic forces and the person being tormented. By using His authority over unclean spirits, Jesus showed that **intercession can break the chains of spiritual bondage** and bring freedom to those oppressed by the enemy.

Jesus' encounters with demonic forces demonstrate that **intercession is not only about prayer but also about taking authority** over the spiritual forces of darkness. His deliverance ministry revealed the **power of God's kingdom** to overthrow the kingdom of darkness. Every time Jesus cast out a demon, it was an act of intercession—He was fighting on behalf of the oppressed, freeing them from spiritual captivity.

Jesus' deliverance ministry was a direct confrontation with the powers of darkness. His intercession was not just a prayer—it was a demonstration of His authority over evil.

In **Mark 5:1-20**, we see the story of the **demon-possessed man in the region of the Gerasenes**. This man was tormented by a legion of demons, living among tombs and causing fear in the community. When Jesus arrived, He interceded for the man by commanding the demons to leave, freeing him from their torment. The man was restored to his right mind, and his life became a testimony to the **power of Jesus' intercessory deliverance**.

Take authority in prayer. When interceding for others, recognize that you have authority in Christ to confront spiritual darkness. Pray for deliverance with confidence, knowing that Jesus has given you power over the forces of the enemy.

Raising the Dead: The Ultimate Act of Intercession

*"Jesus said to her, 'I am the resurrection
and the life. The one who believes in me
will live, even though they die.'" (John 11:25)*

Jesus performed some of His most powerful acts of intercession through **raising the dead**. These miracles were the ultimate demonstration of His authority over life and death, and they pointed to His role as the one who would conquer death through His resurrection. **Raising the dead** was a profound act of intercession because it involved bringing people back from death, overcoming the finality of the grave through the power of God.

From raising **Jairus' daughter** (Mark 5:21-43) to **Lazarus** (John 11), Jesus' authority over death was clear. These miracles showed that **intercession can break through even the most hopeless of situations**. Jesus interceded with the Father on behalf of the dead, and in each case, life was restored. His miracles of resurrection also foreshadowed His own victory over death through the cross and resurrection, offering hope to all who believe in Him.

In raising the dead, Jesus showed that intercession is not bound by time or circumstance. The power of God can reach into the grave and bring life where there is none.

Perhaps the most famous example of Jesus raising the dead is **the story of Lazarus** (John 11:1-44). After hearing of Lazarus' sickness, Jesus delayed His arrival, knowing that Lazarus would die. But when He finally arrived, He declared, *"I am the resurrection and the life,"* and called Lazarus out of the tomb, despite the fact that he had been dead for four days. This act of intercession **revealed the depth of Jesus' authority over death** and His ability to bring life where all hope seemed lost. By raising Lazarus, Jesus demonstrated that **His intercession could reverse even the most irreversible situations**, showing the power of God to restore life.

This miracle was not only a moment of personal triumph for Lazarus and his family but also a **declaration to all who witnessed it**—that in Jesus, life and death are in the hands of God. Through His intercession, Jesus bridged the gap between the power of death and the promise of eternal life.

Believe that no situation is too far gone for God. When interceding for others, even in the face of seemingly impossible circumstances, trust that God can bring life out of death. Just as Jesus raised the dead, God can intervene in hopeless situations to bring about His purposes.

The Cross: The Ultimate Act of Intercession for Humanity

"But He was wounded for our transgressions, He was bruised for our iniquities; the chastisement for our peace was upon Him, and by His stripes we are healed." (Isaiah 53:5)

The ultimate act of intercession by Jesus was His **sacrifice on the cross**. This was not just a moment of suffering—it was the moment when **Jesus stood in the gap for all of humanity**, taking on the punishment of sin and bridging the divide between God and mankind. On the cross, Jesus **interceded for us**, offering Himself as the atoning sacrifice that would bring redemption to all who believe.

Jesus' death on the cross is the foundation of His intercessory ministry. **He bore the sins of the world**, and in doing so, He opened the door for us to receive forgiveness, healing, and eternal life. His intercession didn't end at the cross, though. **Jesus rose from the dead**, proving His victory over sin and death, and He now continually intercedes for us at the right hand of God (Romans 8:34).

The cross is the greatest act of intercession in history. Jesus willingly took our place, bearing our sins, so that we might be reconciled to God. In this, He became the eternal intercessor for humanity.

While hanging on the cross, Jesus continued to intercede for others, even in His final moments. **He prayed for those who crucified Him**, saying, *"Father, forgive them, for they do not know what they are doing"* (Luke 23:34). This powerful act of forgiveness showed that even in the midst of intense suffering, **Jesus' heart was still focused on interceding for those around Him**.

Remember that Jesus' intercession for you is ongoing. Just as He stood in the gap for all humanity on the cross, He continues to intercede for you today. When you pray and intercede for others, draw strength from the fact that Jesus is continually praying for you as well.

Jesus' Ongoing Intercession: Our High Priest in Heaven

"Who then is the one who condemns? No one. Christ Jesus who died—more than that, who was raised to life—is at the right hand of God and is also interceding for us." (Romans 8:34)

Even now, after His ascension, J**esus continues to intercede** for us as our **Great High Priest**. He stands before the Father, praying for us and advocating on our behalf. This role as intercessor is not limited to His earthly ministry; it is a central part of His identity as the **risen Lord**. His ongoing intercession ensures that we have access to the Father, and through His prayers, we are continually strengthened and empowered.

Jesus' role as our **eternal intercessor** means that we are never alone in our struggles or prayers. He is actively involved in our lives, continually lifting us up before the Father and making a way for us to experience God's grace and power. As we intercede for others, we can be encouraged that **Jesus is always interceding for us**.

Jesus' intercession didn't end with His time on earth. He lives forever to intercede for His people, ensuring that we have access to the grace, mercy, and power of God.

The book of Hebrews describes Jesus as our **Great High Priest**, who continually offers prayers and intercession on behalf of His people. This means that **we have a constant advocate** in heaven, ensuring that our prayers are heard and that we have ongoing access to the presence of God.

Rest in the assurance of Jesus' ongoing intercession. As you pray and intercede for others, remember that Jesus is praying for you. He is actively involved in your life, advocating for you before the Father and ensuring that God's grace and power are at work on your behalf.

Jesus, Our Model and Empowerment for Intercession

Throughout His life and ministry, **Jesus modeled intercession** through His prayers, His miracles, and ultimately His sacrifice on the cross. He stood in the gap for the sick, the oppressed, the lost, and all of humanity, demonstrating that **intercession is not just about words—it is about action, compassion, and power**. Every miracle He performed flowed out of His intercessory heart, and every act of healing, deliverance, and even resurrection was a demonstration of God's kingdom breaking into the world through intercession.

As we follow Jesus, we are called to **join Him in His ministry of intercession**. We can intercede for others with confidence, knowing that Jesus is still interceding for us. His life is the perfect example of how intercession is both prayer and action, and it challenges us to **pray with faith** and to expect God's power to be released through our prayers.

Embrace Jesus' example of intercession. As you pray for others, do so with the understanding that intercession involves standing in the gap, believing for miracles, and partnering with God to bring healing, deliverance, and life to those in need. Just as Jesus demonstrated, intercession has the power to transform lives.

Chapter 22

PAUL THE APOSTLE – AN INTERCESSOR EMPOWERED BY SIGNS, WONDERS, AND MIRACLES

Paul's Heart of Intercession

"For God is my witness, whom I serve with my spirit in the gospel of His Son, that without ceasing I make mention of you always in my prayers." —Romans 1:9

Paul the Apostle was one of the most influential figures in the early church, and his ministry was marked by extraordinary **signs, wonders, and miracles**. Yet, beneath the surface of his active ministry lay a profound **heart of intercession**. Paul was not just a preacher or teacher; he was a man deeply invested in the spiritual well-being of the churches he planted and the believers he ministered to. **His letters reveal the depth of his prayer life** and his ongoing concern for the spiritual growth and protection of the early Christians.

Paul's **intercession** was often expressed in the letters he wrote to the churches. Even when he was physically distant from them, he spoke of being **present in spirit** or carrying them in his heart. His prayers for them were not mere formalities but heartfelt petitions, asking God for wisdom, strength, protection, and spiritual growth for those under his care.

The accounts of the miracles that followed Paul's ministry will leave even the most faith filled believer challenged if they consider them earnestly. I can tell you that these things can and do still happen today. I have seen these things happen to people and heard the stories from some of the most sincere individuals. It is often hard to believe until someone you know experiences it. Especially when you know that person has no agenda or motives other than genuinely seeking God.

While in my first year of ministry school I was blessed to live with some of the best and most genuine guys I have ever met. One of them was Abi Abibula, a man from Trinidad. While in school that year he was seen in Trinidad by close relatives on multiple occasions. I have heard these stories from his family firsthand now and it left all of us in wonder. Was it the angelic somehow? Was it Abi himself traveling in Spirit to be around those he "held in his heart"? We aren't entirely sure, but we know it is undeniable that it happened. I also know that this is a man who had his life devoted to the things of God and his mindset and prayer life was focused on Jesus. It is quite possible that he was walking in these things as he began to grow as a believer without fully realizing what spiritual legs he was stretching.

In this chapter, we will explore **Paul's role as an intercessor**, his witness to miracles and signs, and how he maintained a deep spiritual connection with the churches, even from afar.

Paul's Conversion and Calling: The Foundation of His Intercessory Ministry

"For I will show him how much he must suffer for the sake of my name." Acts 9:16

Paul's journey as an intercessor began with his dramatic **conversion on the road to Damascus**. Before this life-changing event, Paul (then Saul) was a zealous persecutor of Christians. However, as he traveled to Damascus to arrest followers of Jesus, he had an **encounter with Christ**, which would forever change the course of his life. Struck blind by the glory of Jesus, Paul heard the voice of the Lord, and through the prayer of **Ananias**, Paul's sight was restored, and he was filled with the Holy Spirit.

This profound encounter with Christ set the stage for **Paul's ministry of intercession**. From the moment of his conversion, Paul's heart burned with a desire to see the gospel spread, and he became deeply committed to **praying for the churches** he would later plant. His transformation from persecutor to apostle is a testimony to the power of prayer and divine intervention, as **God's mercy and the prayers of the saints** played a crucial role in his calling.

Paul's conversion was the result of divine intervention, and from that point on, his life became a testimony to the power of prayer and God's grace.

After his conversion, Paul would go on to become one of the most fervent intercessors in the early church. In his letters, he frequently wrote about how **he prayed constantly** for the believers under his care, asking for their spiritual growth and strength in the face of persecution. **Paul's intercession was birthed from his own experience of grace**, knowing firsthand the power of God's intervention.

Let your own experiences with God fuel your prayers for others. Like Paul, who was transformed through divine intervention, allow your personal encounters with God to deepen your commitment to praying for those in need of His power and grace.

Miracles, Signs, and Wonders: Paul's Intercession in Action

"And God wrought special miracles by the hands of Paul, so that even handkerchiefs or aprons that had touched him were taken to the sick, and their illnesses were cured and the evil spirits left them." —Acts 19:11-12

Paul's ministry was marked by **miracles, signs, and wonders**, which were often the result of his deep **intercessory prayers** and his unwavering faith in the power of the Holy Spirit. **Intercession for Paul was not passive;**

it was active and led to the supernatural intervention of God. Whether healing the sick, casting out demons, or raising the dead, Paul demonstrated that intercession goes hand in hand with the miraculous power of God.

In **Acts 19**, we see that **God worked extraordinary miracles through Paul**, to the point where even handkerchiefs and aprons that had touched him were taken to the sick, and they were healed. This reveals the **depth of Paul's connection with the Holy Spirit**—his life was so saturated with God's power that physical objects carried the anointing for healing and deliverance.

Another notable example of Paul's miracle-working intercession occurred in Acts 14, where, while preaching in Lystra, he saw a man who had been lame from birth. **Paul, perceiving the man's faith, commanded him to stand up, and the man was healed immediately**. This miracle caused great amazement among the people, and it opened the door for the gospel to be preached with power.

"Paul's intercession often took the form of bold, faith-filled actions. His prayers were backed by an expectation that God would move in power, and the signs and wonders that followed his ministry were evidence of God's answer to those prayers."

Perhaps one of the most extraordinary miracles of Paul's ministry was in **Acts 20:9-12**, when a young man named **Eutychus** fell from a third-story window during one of Paul's late-night sermons. The fall killed him, but **Paul immediately went down, embraced the young man, and prayed for him**, raising him from the dead. This act of healing brought Eutychus back to life and encouraged the believers with a powerful demonstration of God's power.

Expect God to move in power through your intercession. Like Paul, walk with the faith to perform miracles, heal the sick, and bring deliverance. Intercession is not just words but an invitation to be saturated in the Spirit.

Paul's Intercessory Heart for the Churches: "Present in Spirit"

"For though I am absent in body, yet I am with you in spirit, rejoicing to see your good order and the firmness of your faith in Christ." (Colossians 2:5)

Paul's deep **love and concern** for the churches he planted is evident throughout his letters. Even when he was physically distant from them, he expressed being **"present in spirit"** with them, interceding for their growth, unity, and perseverance. This was not just a poetic phrase—Paul's **spiritual connection** to these churches was real, and he often described feeling the burden of their spiritual struggles as if he were with them.

In **2 Corinthians 11:28**, Paul wrote about the daily pressure he felt for all the churches, describing how he carried them in his heart. His letters are filled with prayers, encouragements, and reminders of the **constant intercession** he made on their behalf. Paul's intercessory ministry was not limited to the miracles he performed in person but extended across great distances, as he trusted the Holy Spirit to work in the lives of the believers even when he couldn't be physically present.

One powerful example of Paul's intercessory heart is in his letter to the **Thessalonians**. In **1 Thessalonians 3:10**, Paul writes that he prays "night and day most earnestly" for the believers, desiring to see them again and supply what is lacking in their faith. This longing to see the churches flourish spiritually was the driving force behind his prayers, and it reveals his deep commitment to **interceding for their spiritual well-being**.

"Paul's intercessory ministry extended beyond his physical presence. His prayers transcended distance, as he continually lifted up the churches and believers before the throne of God, trusting that the Holy Spirit would guide and protect them."

In **1 Corinthians 5**, Paul addresses a serious moral issue within the church. Though he was not present physically, he wrote that he was **present in spirit** and had already made a judgment, as if he were with them. This demonstrates how Paul's intercession allowed him to remain deeply connected to the spiritual condition of the churches, even when he was not with them in person.

Carry others in your heart through intercessory prayer. Like Paul, even when you are not physically with someone, you can be present in spirit through prayer. As you intercede for others, trust that the Holy Spirit will work powerfully in their lives, even at a distance.

Suffering and Intercession: Paul's Spiritual Travail

"I have great sorrow and unceasing anguish in my heart. For I could wish that I myself were accursed and cut off from Christ for the sake of my brothers, my kinsmen according to the flesh." (Romans 9:2-3)

Paul's intercessory ministry was also marked by **personal suffering** and deep emotional and spiritual travail for the people he ministered to. He often spoke of the **burden** he carried for the churches and the people of Israel. His letters reveal a man who was willing to endure great hardship for the sake of those he prayed for. **Intercession for Paul was not without cost**, and he frequently mentioned the **suffering he endured** as part of his apostolic calling.

In **Romans 9**, Paul writes about his anguish for the Jewish people, expressing that he would be willing to be cut off from Christ if it meant their salvation. This is a profound example of **intercessory love**—Paul was willing to endure great personal loss for the sake of others coming to know Christ.

Paul's willingness to suffer for the sake of the gospel, including his imprisonments, beatings, and hardships, was an extension of his intercessory heart. He understood that **intercession often involves bearing the burdens of others**, both spiritually and physically. His letters to the churches often included requests for prayer, not only for his deliverance but also for the continued **spread of the gospel** and the strengthening of the believers.

"Paul's intercession was costly. He was willing to suffer and even lay down his life for the sake of those he ministered to, embodying the heart of Jesus in his prayers and actions."

In **Philippians 1:19,** Paul expresses his confidence that through the **prayers of the believers** and the help of the Spirit of Jesus Christ, his imprisonment would turn out for his deliverance. Even in prison, Paul was interceding for the churches, and he trusted that their intercession for him would result in his release. This mutual intercession between Paul and the churches illustrates the power of **corporate prayer and spiritual solidarity**.

Be willing to bear the burdens of others in intercession. True intercession often requires a willingness to share in the suffering of those you pray for. Like Paul, pray with a heart that is willing to endure hardship for the sake of others, trusting that God will use your prayers to bring breakthrough and deliverance.

Paul's Legacy of Intercession: A Model for the Church

"I thank my God in all my remembrance of you, always in every prayer of mine for you all making my prayer with joy." (Philippians 1:3-4)

Paul's legacy as an intercessor extends far beyond his time. His letters to the early churches remain some of the most important texts for Christian faith and practice, and they are filled with examples of **fervent intercession, spiritual authority, and supernatural power**. Paul's life serves as a model for the church today—showing us what it means to be an intercessor who prays with faith, believes for miracles, and carries others in the heart with love and commitment.

Paul's intercession was deeply personal. He often wrote of his **love and affection for the believers**, reminding them that he prayed for them constantly. He modeled a life of prayer that was not only focused on **individual needs** but also on the **spiritual growth of the church** as a whole.

Paul's intercession was marked by love, faith, and perseverance. His example challenges the church today to embrace the call to intercede for others with the same fervor and commitment.

In **Ephesians 1:16-23**, Paul offers one of his most beautiful prayers for the church, asking that the believers would receive **a spirit of wisdom and revelation** in the knowledge of God and that they would understand the riches of His glorious inheritance and the immeasurable greatness of His power. This prayer reflects Paul's heart as an intercessor—not just for individual needs, but for the deep spiritual growth of the body of Christ.

Follow Paul's example of intercession. Pray for others with love, commitment, and faith, just as Paul did. Focus not only on immediate needs but also on their spiritual growth and the expansion of what God is doing in their lives.

Chapter 23

INTERCESSION IN THE HEART OF DARKNESS – PRAYING IN HITLER'S OFFICE

The Power of Intercession in Times of War

"For we do not wrestle against flesh and blood, but against principalities, against powers, against the rulers of the darkness of this age, against spiritual hosts of wickedness in the heavenly places." —Ephesians 6:12

During one of the darkest times in modern history—**World War II**, when Adolf Hitler's regime spread terror across Europe—a small group of Norwegian Christians carried out a remarkable act of faith. **Intercessors**, burdened by the weight of Nazi oppression and the suffering it caused, felt called by God to engage in spiritual warfare through prayer. According to faith-based accounts, this group of believers found themselves standing in a place few would ever have imagined: **inside one of the Nazi headquarters**— some say Hitler's office itself.

While the historical details surrounding this event remain limited, the story has become a profound reminder within Christian circles of the power of intercession in the face of evil. Whether in the darkest times of war or the battles we face today, intercession is a powerful weapon that can change the course of history.

The Intercessors: A Call to Spiritual Warfare

"The effective, fervent prayer of a
righteous man avails much." (James 5:16)

The group of **Norwegian intercessors** who prayed during World War II felt an overwhelming burden to pray for their nation, for Europe, and for the downfall of Adolf Hitler's regime. Norway had been occupied by Nazi forces since 1940, and the oppression of the Norwegian people was a constant reality. These believers understood that the war was not only a physical battle but a **spiritual one as well**.

In times of prayer, they felt the leading of the Holy Spirit to pray against the powers of darkness that were manifesting through Hitler's totalitarian regime. These intercessors believed that the only way to combat such a pervasive evil was through persistent, fervent prayer. They were convinced that **God had the power to intervene**, even in a conflict that seemed so overwhelming.

The intercessors knew that in order to stand against the evil of Nazi oppression, they had to engage in spiritual warfare. Their prayers became a shield and a weapon against the spiritual forces working through Hitler's regime.

The courage of these intercessors was fueled by the belief that they were engaged in more than just a political or military battle—they were engaged in a **spiritual struggle**. They knew that their prayers could affect not only the outcome of the war but also the lives of the people suffering under Nazi rule. Their call to intercede was one that many in the church around the world shared, as people of faith recognized that prayer was essential in the fight against the darkness engulfing Europe.

Engage in spiritual warfare through prayer. Just as these intercessors recognized the spiritual battle behind the physical war, we too must understand that many of our struggles are spiritual in nature. Pray with the confidence that your intercession can shift circumstances and push back the forces of darkness.

A Miraculous Entry: Inside Enemy Territory

"The king's heart is in the hand of the Lord; He directs it like a watercourse wherever He pleases." Proverbs 21:1

The most extraordinary part of this story is how these Norwegian intercessors reportedly gained access to a Nazi headquarters. While the exact details remain unclear, the event is often described as a **miracle of divine intervention**, allowing them to enter a place that was usually heavily guarded. Whether through the favor of God, the opening of doors in unexpected ways, or perhaps by blending in under the radar, they found themselves inside a location of profound significance.

Some versions of the story suggest that they were even able to enter **Hitler's office** or another strategic Nazi headquarters, where they felt led by the Spirit to **intercede fervently for the defeat of the regime and the liberation of the oppressed**. The courage it took for them to stand in such a place, knowing the danger they faced, speaks to their deep trust in God's protection and the urgency they felt for the spiritual battle they were engaged in.

Standing in the heart of enemy territory, these intercessors took their place before God, praying not only for the fall of Hitler's regime but also for the protection and salvation of the countless lives at risk during the war.

Imagine the scene: A group of Christians, aware of the overwhelming power and evil that Nazi Germany represented, standing in what they believed to be **the very place where decisions of destruction were made**. Yet, instead of fear, they felt the **presence of God** with them, knowing that their prayers in that moment could change the course of history. Their prayer was an act of resistance, a defiant stand against the darkness through the light of Christ.

Take bold steps in faith, even when the odds seem impossible. Like the intercessors who found themselves praying in Hitler's office, sometimes God calls us into situations where we must trust Him fully. Pray boldly, knowing that God can place you in the right place at the right time to accomplish His will.

Interceding in the Presence of Evil:
Prayers of Faith and Resistance

"The light shines in the darkness, and the darkness has not overcome it." John 1:5

Inside the Nazi headquarters, the intercessors began to pray fervently. Their prayers were not just petitions—they were acts of **spiritual warfare**. They prayed for the defeat of Hitler's plans, for the end of Nazi oppression, and for the liberation of those under the regime's control. They interceded on behalf of the millions of Jews, prisoners, and innocent civilians who were suffering and dying across Europe.

In that moment, they were aware of the intense **spiritual battle** taking place. Nazi ideology was not just a political force—it was deeply tied to darkness, hatred, and evil. The intercessors understood that they were confronting **principalities and powers**, and they prayed with the full confidence that God's power was greater than anything the Nazi regime could muster.

It is said that while they prayed, the intercessors felt a **supernatural peace**, even as they stood in the midst of one of the most evil regimes in modern history. They believed that the darkness they faced was no match for the **light of Christ** and that their prayers, though spoken in a seemingly impossible situation, were being heard in the courts of heaven. They prayed with faith that **God would intervene**.

Pray with faith in the face of evil. Even when you find yourself in dark or seemingly hopeless situations, trust that your prayers have power. Just as these intercessors prayed in the heart of Nazi Germany, we too can stand in the gap and pray for God's intervention in even the darkest of circumstances.

The Power of Intercession:
Changing the Course of History

"If my people, who are called by my name, will humble themselves and pray and seek my face and turn from their wicked ways, then I will hear from heaven, and I will forgive their sin and will heal their land." (2 Chronicles 7:14)

Though we may never know the full extent of how the prayers of these intercessors impacted the war, their story serves as a powerful example of the **role of intercession in changing history**. They believed that their prayers, offered in faith, could influence the course of events in ways that went far beyond what human effort could achieve.

The end of World War II came in 1945, and Hitler's regime was defeated. While many factors contributed to the Allies' victory, stories like these remind us that **God's hand was at work, and that prayer played a critical role** in the spiritual battle that raged during those years. The intercessors who prayed during the war may have never seen the full results of their prayers, but they stood firm in their belief that **God heard them and acted**.

The prayers of these intercessors were like seeds planted in the soil of history. Though they may not have seen the full harvest, their faith and intercession played a part in God's greater plan for the defeat of Nazi Germany.

Intercession during wartime has often been a practice in the church. Throughout history, from **Moses interceding for Israel** to modern-day prayer movements, intercessors have stood in the gap, believing that their prayers can shift nations, end wars, and change the course of **history**. Just like these Norwegian intercessors, people of faith throughout the ages have understood that, while wars are fought with weapons on the ground, they are often won through prayer in the heavens. The victory over Nazi Germany, and the liberation of millions from oppression, was undoubtedly

influenced by the **prayers of countless intercessors** who stood in the gap
during the war.

 Your prayers matter, even if you don't see the immediate results.
The intercessors who prayed during World War II may not have seen the
full impact of their prayers, but they prayed with faith that God would work.
Trust that your intercession plays a part in God's greater plan, even if the
results are not immediately visible.

A Legacy of Intercession: What We Can Learn Today

"Pray without ceasing." (1 Thessalonians 5:17)

 The story of the **Norwegian intercessors** who prayed in Nazi
headquarters during World War II reminds us of the enduring power of
intercession. It teaches us that **prayer is not bound by circumstances** or
limited by physical realities. Whether we are praying for an end to war, for
the healing of our nation, or for individuals trapped in darkness, **our prayers
reach the throne of God** and can affect real change.

 In the same way that these intercessors stood in the gap during one
of the darkest periods in history, we are called to stand in the gap for our
generation. The battles may look different, but the spiritual principles
remain the same. **Intercession is a powerful tool in the hands of believers**,
and it can shift the course of nations, bring down evil regimes, and protect
the innocent.

 The legacy of these intercessors lives on in the lives of those who
continue to pray today. Their story encourages us to **pray boldly, even when
the odds seem impossible**, and to trust that God is able to do exceedingly
abundantly above all that we ask or think (Ephesians 3:20).

 *The legacy of these intercessors is not just about what they did during
World War II—it's about the faith they carried and the belief that prayer
could change the world. That same faith is available to us today.*

 The faith of these intercessors can inspire us to pray in our own
challenging situations. Whether it's praying for peace in conflict zones,
interceding for oppressed people groups, or praying for revival in our cities,

we are part of the same legacy of intercessors who believe that God moves through prayer. Just as they stood firm in their prayers during a time of war, we too can stand firm in prayer, trusting that God will act on behalf of His people.

Be part of the legacy of intercession. Like the Norwegian intercessors who prayed during World War II, commit yourself to a life of prayer. Believe that your intercession can affect real change, whether in your community, your nation, or the world.

Intercession in Dark Times – A Call to Prayer

The story of the **Norwegian intercessors** who prayed in the midst of Nazi Germany is a powerful testimony to the belief that **prayer can change the world**. They stood in the gap, even in the heart of enemy territory, and prayed with faith that God would intervene in the war and bring an end to the evil they saw around them.

Though the details of their story may remain somewhat unclear, the lesson is unmistakable: **intercession matters**. Whether we are praying for world-changing events or for the everyday battles we face, God hears our prayers. The same power that worked through the prayers of these intercessors is available to us today.

As we reflect on their legacy, we are reminded of the importance of standing in prayer during times of darkness. **Prayer is our most powerful weapon**, and when we engage in intercession, we invite God's presence and power into the world. Just as these intercessors prayed for the defeat of Hitler's regime, we too can pray for God's kingdom to come and His will to be done on earth as it is in heaven.

Commit to a life of intercession. Let the story of the Norwegian intercessors inspire you to pray with boldness and faith. Believe that your prayers can change the course of history and that God is ready to move when His people call upon Him.

Unfortunately, there are no verifiable or historically documented sources that specifically detail the **Norwegian intercessors** praying in **Hitler's office** during World War II. This story has primarily been circulated in **Christian oral traditions** and faith-based accounts but is not backed by direct historical evidence. While it serves as an inspiring narrative in some spiritual communities about the power of intercession, there are no primary historical documents or academic sources to substantiate this particular event.

For historically documented instances of **Christian resistance** and prayer movements during World War II, you might want to look into:

1. The Confessing Church in Germany, which included notable figures like **Dietrich Bonhoeffer** and **Karl Barth,** who resisted Nazi ideology through prayer, theology, and underground activities.

2. The Resistance in Norway during the Nazi occupation, which included various acts of defiance and support for the Allied cause, though prayer and intercession movements within these groups are not as clearly documented.

3. Intercession movements during World War II, where Christians around the world prayed for victory against the Axis powers and for peace.

For more general resources on Christian intercession during times of war or spiritual warfare, here are some useful books and articles:

- **Bonhoeffer: Pastor, Martyr, Prophet, Spy by Eric Metaxas** – A biography of Dietrich Bonhoeffer, a theologian who was deeply involved in resisting Hitler's regime.

- **God in the Shadows: Evil in God's World by Brian Morley** – Provides insight into Christian theology on evil and the role of intercession in times of great darkness.

- **Hitler's** Cross by **Erwin Lutzer** – Explores how the church in Nazi Germany responded to Hitler and the spiritual dynamics at play.

For now, the story of the **Norwegian intercessors** remains an inspiring narrative within the realm of faith tradition, without direct historical backing. It should be shared and remembered as an example of the importance of prayer and intercession, while keeping in mind the lack of hard documentation.

Chapter 24

THE BOOK OF HEBREWS – THE CALL TO DEEPER THINGS

The Higher Life in Christ

The Book of Hebrews stands as one of the most profound revelations of the **Christian faith**. It's not merely a letter—it's a call. A call to leave behind the shadows of the old covenant and press into the **deeper, fuller life in Christ,** a life that transcends mere ritual and religion and takes us into the very heart of **God's power and presence**. It is a summons to rise higher, to see with spiritual eyes, and to walk in the fullness of the **inheritance Christ has purchased** for His people.

Hebrews is the voice of the Spirit speaking to believers who may have grown content with the **elementary things** of faith, calling them into maturity. The writer implores us to move beyond the veil, to enter into the **Holy of Holies**—not just through intellectual understanding but through **living union with Christ**, the high priest of a new and living covenant. This book reveals the **superiority of Christ** over all things and invites us into a participation in His divine life.

Jesus, the Fulfillment of All Things

The central theme of Hebrews is the **supremacy of Jesus Christ**. Paul speaks to a people who had known the law, who had grown familiar with the temple and its sacrifices. These were good things, given by God, but they were shadows of something greater. Hebrews begins by declaring, *"In the past God spoke to our ancestors through the prophets at many times and in various ways, but in these last days He has spoken to us by His Son"* (Hebrews 1:1-2).

What Paul is saying here is this: **Jesus is the final Word**. He is the fulfillment of every prophetic utterance, every sacrifice, every ritual. The old system was temporary, designed to point us toward the **greater reality of Christ**. When Jesus came, He did not come merely to establish another religious system; He came to bring us into the **living experience of God Himself**.

Jesus is described as the **"radiance of God's glory and the exact representation of His being"** (Hebrews 1:3). This means that to see Jesus is to see the **heart of the Father** revealed in fullness. He is not a shadow of something greater—He is the **reality** to which the shadows point. And what did Jesus do? He didn't just talk about access to God; **He made it possible**. He is our **High Priest** and **our perfect sacrifice**. In Him, every wall of separation has been torn down, and we are invited to live in the fullness of that divine communion.

God has called you to the reality of Himself in Christ, not just as a doctrine or theology, but as the living, breathing experience of the fullness of His Spirit.

A Call to Maturity: Pressing Beyond the Basics

In Hebrews 5 and 6, Paul issues a strong challenge to believers: **Move on to maturity**. He tells the recipients that they should already be teachers by now, but they are still in need of **spiritual milk** (Hebrews 5:12). He's not condemning them for needing to start with the basics—he's calling them to **rise higher**.

Paul speaks of the **"elementary teachings about Christ"**—repentance from dead works, faith in God, baptisms, laying on of hands, resurrection of the dead, and eternal judgment (Hebrews 6:1-2). These are foundational truths, but they are not the end. The believer's life is meant to grow into the deeper things of God.

I have often heard this verse used as an excuse to belittle those aforementioned things. However, take into consideration for a moment, the placement of this book in the Bible. I don't believe that the order of the New Testament books is any accident. You start with the Good News, move into the works of the Spirit and the apostles, then you are taken through the process of the early church beginning to grow and walk out their faith. I believe the Author of this book is saying that everything up and to that point is the elementary teachings and practices. The milk is great but lets grow to be strong and advance in our maturity! This book is inviting us into the next level, if we will have the eyes to see and ears to hear.

We were not saved simply to escape judgment—we were saved to **enter into union with God**. And here is the deeper call of Hebrews: You are not meant to remain at the outer courts, lingering around the **shadows of the temple**. You are called into the **Holy of Holies**, where the full light of Christ shines. You are called to **spiritual maturity**, to live not just in the knowledge of Christ but in the power of **His resurrection**.

The church today must hear this call. Many have been satisfied with **religious forms**—attending services, reading Scriptures, and participating in rituals—but the time has come for the **fullness of Christ's life** to be manifest in us. We are to **lay hold** of the **full inheritance** Christ has made available, moving beyond the elementary principles and stepping into the deeper realities of His Spirit.

There is a deeper life in God that many have yet to touch. It is the life of the Spirit where Christ lives fully in you, where His power flows through you, and where His presence transforms the world around you.

Entering Into the Rest of God

One of the most powerful themes in Hebrews is the call to enter into **God's rest**. In Hebrews 4, Paul reminds the people of Israel's failure to enter the promised land because of their unbelief. They wandered in the wilderness, but the **rest of God** was still available to them. Paul then declares that this **rest remains** for the people of God (Hebrews 4:9).

What is this rest? It is the **rest of faith**—the place where we cease from striving in our own strength and **fully trust** in what Christ has accomplished. This rest is not inactivity; it is living in the **finished work of Jesus**, where we are no longer striving to be holy or acceptable to God. In Christ, we have been made holy, and now we are called to **live from that place of rest**.

This is a challenge to every believer. Many are still laboring under the burden of trying to please God through their own works, trying to earn His favor or maintain His approval. But **Hebrews shouts the truth**: You cannot earn what Christ has already given. The **finished work of the cross** is the doorway into this rest. When we live in this place, **God's power flows through us unhindered**, because we are no longer striving but resting in His grace.

The rest of God is the place of spiritual power and freedom. It is where the Christian ceases from striving and enters into the life of Christ, where His works flow through you effortlessly.

The New Covenant: Living Beyond the Veil

In Hebrews 8, Paul declares that **Jesus is the mediator of a new and better covenant** (Hebrews 8:6). The old covenant, with its laws, sacrifices, and rituals, was only a **shadow** of what was to come. In Christ, we have entered into the **reality**. This new covenant is based not on **our works** but on the finished work of Christ, who offered Himself as the perfect sacrifice once and for all (Hebrews 10:12-14).

What does this mean for the believer? It means that the **veil has been torn** (Hebrews 10:19-20). In the old covenant, the Holy of Holies was separated by a thick veil, and only the high priest could enter once a year to offer sacrifices. But now, in Christ, we have **bold access** to the very presence of God. We are no longer distant from Him—we are invited to live in **intimate fellowship** with Him.

Living in this **new covenant reality** is not just about forgiveness of sins, though that is part of it. It is about living in **full communion** with the Spirit of God, walking daily in His power and presence. The life of the believer is meant to be lived beyond the veil, where the **supernatural becomes natural**, where the life of God flows through us, and where we **participate in the divine nature** (2 Peter 1:4).

Fixing Our Eyes on Jesus: The Author and Finisher of Our Faith

Finally, Hebrews calls us to **fix our eyes on Jesus**. In chapter 12, Paul exhorts believers to **run the race** with endurance, looking to Jesus, the **author and finisher** of our faith (Hebrews 12:1-2). This is the ultimate call to the deeper life: **Christ Himself**.

We are not called to look to the law, to rituals, or to religious systems. We are called to look to **Jesus**, the One who began this work in us and the One who will bring it to completion. As we press into the deeper things of God, our eyes must remain fixed on Him. It is His life in us that transforms us. It is His Spirit that empowers us. And it is His love that sustains us.

The deeper things of God are not reserved for a select few. They are available to all who will pursue Him, all who will respond to the call of Hebrews to **go deeper, to live fully in the reality of Christ's presence and power**.

Chapter 25

JOHN, THE APOSTLE OF LOVE – RUNNING WITH JESUS TO THE END

The Beloved Disciple

The apostle John is often remembered as the "**disciple whom Jesus loved**." This simple phrase, found several times in the Gospel of John, might seem like a passing detail, but it reveals something profound about John's life and relationship with Jesus. More than any other disciple, **John was defined by love**—both by the love he had for Jesus and the deep awareness of **Jesus' love for him**.

John's unique connection with Jesus wasn't simply a result of proximity or privilege; it was the result of a **heart transformed by love**. From the beginning, John's love for Christ compelled him to stay near Jesus in His most critical moments. It gave him the strength to follow Jesus to the cross when others fled, and it propelled him to run with greater fervency and passion toward the **empty tomb** on the morning of the resurrection.

As the one who leaned on Jesus' chest at the Last Supper, the one who stayed with Him at the cross, and the one who ultimately received the **Revelation of Jesus Christ** on the island of Patmos, John's life is a testimony to the **transforming power** of love and the way that love draws us closer to God's heart.

It wasn't John's love for God but it was the revelation and understanding of Jesus' love for Him that is what sets John apart. I believe this is a key for all of us as we read scripture.

As I've sat under deferent ministries and leaders, there is a common thread I notice. When I see someone who is really walking out their faith in a way that is captivating to me, regardless of theology or background, I have noticed this one theme in their teaching: friendship with God. I believe that is what is offered to us through Jesus Christ. And the next door after that one is to have a full understanding of His love for us. To know it and experience it.

John's Identity: The Disciple Whom Jesus Loved

"One of His disciples, whom Jesus loved, was reclining at the table at Jesus' side." (John 13:23)

Throughout the Gospel of John, we repeatedly encounter this phrase, "the disciple whom Jesus loved." It's important to note that this is not a title given to John by others—it's how **John describes himself**. What a profound revelation! John's identity was so rooted in the **love of Jesus** that, of all the ways he could describe himself, he chose to define his life by **Jesus' love for him**.

This wasn't a statement of superiority or favoritism, as if John were saying he was the only one Jesus loved. Instead, it was the fruit of **John's personal experience** of being loved by Christ. John understood, more deeply than perhaps any of the other disciples, the central role that love played in his relationship with Jesus. He had encountered the love of God in such a powerful way that it shaped his entire life.

In his letters, John would later write, *"We love because He first loved us"* (1 John 4:19). This wasn't just a theological idea for John—it was his lived experience. He knew firsthand that his ability to love others, and even to love Jesus, came from the **overflow of Jesus' love for him**.

John's identity was not wrapped up in his achievements, his position, or his knowledge—it was rooted in the unshakable truth that he was loved by Jesus. That love was the foundation of everything he did.

At the Last Supper, we see John reclining at the table, **resting his head on Jesus' chest** (John 13:23). This intimate moment captures John's closeness to Jesus. While the other disciples were debating who among them would betray Jesus, John was focused on being **near to Jesus' heart**. This closeness wasn't just about physical proximity—it reflected the deep bond of love that existed between them.

Root your identity in the love of Christ. Like John, don't define yourself by what you can accomplish or how others see you. Let your life be defined by the unshakable truth that you are loved by Jesus. From that place, everything else flows.

Love That Stays: John at the Cross

"When Jesus saw His mother there, and the disciple whom He loved standing nearby, He said to her, 'Woman, here is your son,' and to the disciple, 'Here is your mother.'" (John 19:26-27)

When we think about the crucifixion, it's easy to focus on the **suffering of Jesus** and the scattering of His disciples. Yet in the midst of that painful moment, there is one disciple who remains close: **John**. While Peter, James, and the others fled in fear, John stayed with Jesus to the end, standing at the foot of the cross.

What made John stay when the others ran? It wasn't that John had more courage or less fear. It was **love**. John's deep, abiding love for Jesus gave him the strength to remain, even when it was dangerous, even when the sight of Jesus' suffering must have been unbearable. **Love compels us to remain when others walk away**.

At the cross, Jesus entrusted His mother, Mary, into John's care, saying, *"Here is your mother"* (John 19:27). This moment is profound. Of all the disciples, Jesus chose John, the disciple of love, to care for His mother. This act was not just about physical protection—it was about **spiritual closeness**. Jesus recognized the depth of John's love and entrusted him with this sacred responsibility.

Love gives us the strength to stay close to Jesus, even in moments of suffering and pain. John's love for Christ anchored him at the cross, where others had fled in fear. This is a prime example of "perfect love casting out fear".

At the cross, John didn't have answers. He couldn't stop the suffering, and he couldn't make sense of why it was happening. But he stayed. Sometimes love means simply **remaining present**—staying close to Jesus in moments of pain, trusting in His love even when we don't understand.

Love stays, even when it's hard. John's love for Jesus kept him close at the cross. In your own life, love will give you the strength to remain faithful, even in the face of pain or uncertainty. Stay close to Jesus, no matter what comes.

Love That Runs: John at the Empty Tomb

"So Peter and the other disciple started for the tomb. Both were running, but the other disciple outran Peter and reached the tomb first." (John 20:3-4)

The morning of the resurrection is one of the most significant moments in history. When Mary Magdalene came to tell the disciples that Jesus' tomb was empty, **John and Peter** immediately set out running to see for themselves. What's interesting is that John, **motivated by love**, outran Peter and reached the tomb first.

This detail may seem small, but it's significant. **Love gives us motivation**. It propels us toward Jesus with an urgency and passion that no one else can match. John, who had stayed close to Jesus in His suffering, was now the first to run toward Him in His resurrection. His love for Jesus wasn't passive—it was **active**, driving him to be near Jesus in every moment, whether in death or life.

When John reached the tomb and saw the empty linens, he didn't need to see the risen Jesus to believe. **He believed immediately** (John 20:8). This faith, born out of love, allowed John to be one of the first witnesses to the resurrection. **Love and faith are always connected**—when we know that we are loved, we find it easier to trust, to believe, and to run toward Jesus.

Love gives us the courage to run faster, to believe more quickly, and to see more clearly. John's love for Jesus propelled him to the empty tomb and allowed him to believe without hesitation.

The image of John running to the tomb, his heart beating with anticipation and love, captures the urgency of love. When you love someone deeply, you don't delay—you run to be near them. John's love for Jesus gave him the speed to reach the tomb first, and his faith allowed him to believe that Jesus had risen.

Let love propel you toward Jesus. Just as John ran toward the empty tomb, let your love for Jesus drive you toward Him with passion and urgency. When you know you are loved by Him, you will find the strength to run faster and believe more deeply.

The Revelation of Jesus Christ: Love That Receives

"The revelation from Jesus Christ, which
God gave Him to show His servants what
must soon take place." (Revelation 1:1)

In John's later years, after he had faithfully served Jesus for decades, he was **exiled to the island of Patmos**. It was there, in isolation and suffering, that John received the Revelation of Jesus Christ—the final and complete vision of Jesus as the **Alpha and Omega**, the **King of Kings**, and the **victorious Lord** who reigns over all.

John, the disciple who had leaned on Jesus' chest, who had stayed with Him at the cross, and who had run to the empty tomb, was now entrusted with the **full revelation** of Jesus' majesty and glory. It's no accident that John, the disciple of love, was the one chosen to receive this vision. **Love opens the heart to receive revelation.**

John's love for Jesus had carried him through every season. And this is only because Jesus' love for John had carried him through every season.

The Invitation to Intimately Know Jesus: From Love to Intercession

"I am the vine; you are the branches. If you remain in me and I in you, you will bear much fruit; apart from me you can do nothing." (John 15:5)

The life of the apostle John invites us into something far deeper than simply knowing about Jesus—it invites us into a place of **intimate relationship** where we truly know and are known by Him. John's entire life was a demonstration of what it means to be rooted in love, and his closeness to Jesus was the foundation of everything he accomplished in his life.

What we see in John is that **intimacy with Jesus naturally leads to intercession**. The more John knew Jesus—His heart, His love, His desires— the more he was able to **share in the work of Christ**, including standing in the gap for others. Intercession is not merely about praying for people from a distance; it's about drawing near to Jesus and allowing His **compassion, power, and will** to flow through us.

John's closeness to Jesus wasn't just for his own benefit—it positioned him to be a **vessel through which God could reveal Himself to the world**. John's life shows us that the more we abide in Jesus, the more we will find ourselves drawn into the ministry of **intercession**. In John's writings, especially in his Gospel and epistles, we see that **love and prayer go hand in hand**. To love deeply is to pray deeply, and to know Jesus intimately is to share in His ongoing work of interceding for the world.

The invitation to intimately know Jesus is not just about personal transformation—it is a call to stand in the place of intercession, where His love compels us to pray for the world, for the lost, and for the broken.

John at the Cross – Sharing in Jesus' Heart

At the cross, we see perhaps the clearest connection between **intimacy and intercession**. John's closeness to Jesus, his love for Him, gave him the strength to stay with Jesus during His suffering. But more than that, it opened the door for John to share in Jesus' heart for others. As John stood at the foot of the cross, he not only witnessed Jesus' suffering—he was entrusted with Jesus' most precious earthly relationship: **His mother**. Jesus said to John, *"Here is your mother,"* and from that hour, John took her into his home (John 19:27).

This was more than a practical act of care; it was an act of **spiritual intercession**. By remaining close to Jesus in His most painful moment, John was given a deeper understanding of Christ's love and was invited to **carry that love forward by caring for others**. John stood in the place of love, and from that place, he was able to carry the burdens of others, just as Jesus did. In the same way, as we draw closer to Jesus, we are invited to **stand in the gap for others**, to carry their needs, their pain, and their burdens to the Lord in prayer.

Intimacy with Jesus fuels intercession. The closer you are to Jesus, the more your heart will reflect His. As you draw near to Him, you will naturally begin to share in His burden for others, and intercession will flow out of that place of love. **Pray from the heart of Jesus**, knowing that His love for the world compels us to stand in the gap and seek healing, salvation, and restoration for those around us.

Intercession as Participation in Jesus' Mission

"Therefore He is also able to save to the uttermost those who come to God through Him, since He always lives to make intercession for them." (Hebrews 7:25)

John's life reveals to us a powerful truth: **intercession is a continuation of Jesus' mission**. Jesus is not only our Savior; He is our **intercessor**. Hebrews 7:25 tells us that even now, Jesus is continually interceding for us at the right hand of the Father. His work didn't end with His resurrection—

it continues through His intercession, and we are invited to **join in this ministry**.

John, as the apostle of love, understood that to love Jesus meant to participate in His work of intercession. This is why he was entrusted with the **Revelation of Jesus Christ** on the island of Patmos. John's love for Jesus positioned him to receive the **full vision** of Jesus' victorious return and the final restoration of all things. His closeness to Christ allowed him to see **God's ultimate plan** for humanity, and that revelation fueled his prayers and his witness.

In the same way, when we draw close to Jesus, we are invited to share in His mission to bring salvation, healing, and redemption to the world. **Intercession is not just about asking God for things—it's about partnering with Him in His ongoing work**. When we pray, we are not praying our own desires; we are praying **from the heart of Jesus**, standing with Him as He intercedes for the world.

Intercession is the way we join in Jesus' ongoing work. It's the way we partner with Him in His mission to save, heal, and restore the world. When we pray, we are participating in the work of Christ.

John's Vision on Patmos – Intercession through Revelation

When John received the Revelation of Jesus Christ on Patmos, it wasn't just a vision of the future—it was a **call to intercession**. John saw the victory of Jesus, the final defeat of evil, and the restoration of God's people. This vision wasn't given to John just for information—it was given to fuel **prayer and perseverance**. John's revelation allowed him to pray with greater understanding and to **intercede for the church**, knowing that Jesus' victory was certain.

As we spend time in prayer, God may also give us glimpses of His heart, His plans, and His desires for our world. These revelations are not just for our benefit; they are meant to guide our prayers and deepen our intercession. Just as John was given the revelation of Christ's return, we too can receive revelation as we intercede, standing in the gap for others and participating in God's plan for the world.

Intercession is joining Jesus in His ongoing work. When we pray, we are partnering with Christ in His mission to bring salvation, healing, and restoration to the world. Draw near to Him, and let His heart shape your prayers. **You are not praying alone—Jesus is interceding with you**.

Love That Leads to Intercession

John's life is a powerful reminder that **intimacy with Jesus leads to intercession**. His identity as the "disciple whom Jesus loved" shaped every aspect of his life. From the Last Supper to the cross, from the empty tomb to the island of Patmos, John's closeness to Jesus positioned him to **receive revelation**, to remain faithful in times of suffering, and to participate in Jesus' mission through prayer.

The same invitation is extended to us today. As we grow in our **intimate knowledge of Jesus**, we are drawn into His heart for the world. **Intercession flows from that place of love**—it is our response to knowing and being known by Jesus. Just as John ran to the tomb, remained at the cross, and received the Revelation of Christ, we too are called to **run toward Jesus**, to stay close to Him in every season, and to join Him in His work of interceding for others.

When we intercede, we are not praying from a distance. We are **praying from the heart of Jesus**, standing with Him as He continues to intercede for the world. And as we pray, we participate in His mission, bringing His love, healing, and redemption to the world.

"The call to intimacy with Jesus is a call to intercession. As we draw near to Him, we begin to share His heart for the world, and we are invited to stand in the gap, bringing His love, healing, and redemption to those around us."

Chapter 26

THE TABERNACLE OF MOSES
AND THE HOLY OF HOLIES

A Divine Blueprint

The Tabernacle of Moses, described in the book of Exodus, was not merely a physical structure—it was a **divinely designed blueprint** for worship, intimacy with God, and His dwelling among His people. It served as a tangible representation of God's desire to be present with humanity, offering a glimpse of heavenly realities.

Constructed during Israel's wilderness journey, the Tabernacle was a portable sanctuary divided into three sections: the **Outer Court**, the **Holy Place**, and the **Holy of Holies**. Each section had distinct purposes, and the progression through these spaces mirrored humanity's approach to God— beginning with cleansing and sacrifice and culminating in communion with His presence.

At the center of this divine design was the **Holy of Holies**, the most sacred space where the Ark of the Covenant rested, and God's glory dwelled. This chapter explores the structure, symbolism, and deeper significance of the Tabernacle, including the role of numbers in revealing its divine purpose.

From the very beginning, God has desired to dwell with His people. He walked with Adam and Eve in the cool of the garden. He spoke face-to-face with Abraham. And in the wilderness, as the children of Israel journeyed from slavery in Egypt to the Promised Land, God gave them a tangible sign of His presence—the Tabernacle.

The **Tabernacle of Moses** wasn't just a tent. It was a sacred meeting place, designed by God Himself, where His glory could dwell among His people. But it wasn't just a structure—it was a message. Every detail of the Tabernacle pointed to something far greater: God's plan to redeem humanity and bring us into His presence.

A Place of Approach

The Tabernacle was divided into three parts: the **Outer Court**, the **Holy Place**, and the **Holy of Holies**. Each section showed a progression—a journey toward intimacy with God. But let's not miss this: before anyone could enter the Tabernacle, they had to start in the Outer Court, where sacrifices were made.

In the Outer Court, the **Bronze Altar** stood as a reminder that sin separates us from God. A sacrifice had to be offered for sin, and blood had to be shed. It was here that people were reminded of the seriousness of sin and the need for atonement. The **Bronze Laver**, a basin filled with water, stood nearby as a symbol of cleansing. Before a priest could minister on behalf of the people, he had to be cleansed.

This is the starting point for all of us. The Bible says, *"Without the shedding of blood, there is no forgiveness of sins"* (Hebrews 9:22). In the Tabernacle, the blood of animals was offered, but today, we have something far greater. Jesus Christ, the Lamb of God, gave His life for us, so we could be cleansed, forgiven, and made new.

A Place of Worship

Once inside the **Holy Place**, the priests ministered before God. This wasn't a place for casual visitors; it was sacred. The **Golden Lampstand**, with its seven branches, burned continuously, symbolizing the light of

God's Word and the presence of His Spirit. The **Table of Showbread** held twelve loaves of bread, representing God's covenant with His people and His faithful provision. The **Altar of Incense**, placed before the veil, filled the air with the fragrance of prayers ascending to heaven.

This was a place of worship, but it was also a reminder. Worship is not about what we can bring to God—it's about what He has already given us. His light guides us. His provision sustains us. And our prayers, lifted in faith, are a sweet aroma to Him.

Let me ask you: Are you letting God's light guide your steps? Are you trusting in His provision? Are you lifting your heart to Him in prayer? The Holy Place reminds us that worship isn't confined to a building. It's a way of life—walking with God, trusting Him, and praising Him in every moment.

A Place of Presence

Beyond the veil was the most sacred place of all—the **Holy of Holies**. This was where the Ark of the Covenant rested, the very place where God's glory dwelled. Inside the Ark were three items: the Ten **Commandments**, reminding the people of God's law; a jar of **manna**, symbolizing God's provision; and Aaron's **rod that budded**, a sign of God's authority.

But what made the Holy of Holies unique wasn't what was inside the Ark. It was the **Mercy Seat**, the golden cover where the blood of atonement was sprinkled once a year by the high priest. The Mercy Seat represented God's grace, His forgiveness, and His presence among His people.

Here's the good news: you and I don't have to stand outside the veil anymore. The Bible says that the very moment that Jesus died on the cross, the veil in the temple was torn from top to bottom (Matthew 27:51). God Himself tore that veil, opening the way for all of us to enter His presence. We don't need a human priest to stand between us and God. Through Jesus, we can approach the throne of grace with confidence.

The Numbers Speak

Even the dimensions and design of the Tabernacle tell a story. The **number three**, seen in the three sections of the Tabernacle, represents the completeness of God—Father, Son, and Holy Spirit. The **number seven**, symbolized in the Menorah, speaks of perfection and God's finished work.

The **number twelve**, seen in the loaves of bread, points to God's covenant and His faithfulness to His people.

And don't miss this: the Tabernacle was designed as a perfect rectangle, a symbol of balance and order. Every measurement, every material, every instruction had meaning. Why? Because God doesn't do anything by accident. He is a God of order, purpose, and precision. When He gave Moses the plans for the Tabernacle, He was showing us that He has a plan for every detail of our lives.

Fulfilled in Jesus

The Tabernacle of Moses wasn't meant to be permanent. It was a shadow, a glimpse of something greater. Every sacrifice, every symbol, every part of the Tabernacle pointed to Jesus Christ.

- He is the **Lamb of God**, who takes away the sin of the world (John 1:29).
- He is the **Light of the World**, who guides us in darkness (John 8:12).
- He is the **Bread of Life**, who sustains us (John 6:35).
- He is our **High Priest**, who intercedes for us (Hebrews 4:14-16).
- And He is the **Veil**, torn so that we can enter God's presence (Hebrews 10:19-20).

Today, we don't need a physical Tabernacle, because God has made His home in the hearts of those who believe in Him. The Bible says, *"Don't you know that you yourselves are God's temple and that God's Spirit dwells in your midst?"* (1 Corinthians 3:16). Through Jesus, you and I become living Tabernacles, carrying His presence everywhere we go.

The Tabernacle teaches us two things: God is holy, and God is near. He is not distant, hidden, or unapproachable. Through Jesus, He has made a way for us to draw near to Him. The question is: will you come?

If you've been carrying the weight of sin, let me tell you that Jesus has already paid the price. If you've been searching for peace, let me tell you that

His presence can fill your heart. If you've been wondering how to draw close to God, let me tell you that the way has already been opened.

The Tabernacle was a shadow, but the reality is found in Christ. He is inviting you into His presence today. Will you respond?

For further reading on this subject I highly recommend: Unveiling Revelation By Jeremy Butrous. He approaches scripture with clarity, scholarship, and spiritual insight. Rather than leaving the reader overwhelmed by symbolism and imagery, he walks through each section methodically, highlighting the text's central message of hope, redemption, and the ultimate triumph of Jesus Christ. By placing scripture in its proper historical and literary context, he equips believers with the tools to interpret its visions, prophecies, and symbolism in a way that nurtures faith rather than fear.

At the heart of **Unveiling Revelation** is the conviction that scripture is not meant to be a puzzle left unsolved but an unveiling of God's eternal plan. Through accessible language, real-life applications, and a focus on Christ's sovereignty, Butrous invites readers to move beyond confusion and into a place of confident understanding. He underscores that Revelation, for all its complexity, is fundamentally about worship, spiritual victory, and the assurance that God's purposes will prevail. In doing so, **Unveiling Revelation** becomes a transformative resource, helping individuals not only comprehend this profound biblical text but also emerge with a renewed sense of hope, purpose, and expectancy for what is to come.

Chapter 27

THE THRONE ROOM OF GOD – THE INTERSECTION OF POWER, PRESENCE, AND PURPOSE

A Heavenly Reality that Transcends Comprehension

I n the New Testament, the **Throne Room of God** is presented as a place of unmatched power, majesty, and holiness. It is where God reigns in sovereign authority over the universe, where His glory is fully revealed, and where heavenly worship and intercession take place.

The idea of the **Throne Room of God** is not some distant, mystical realm, removed from our everyday experience. No, it is a **present reality**, alive with power, order, and divine authority. The Throne Room is not just a concept for theologians to debate—it is a place where we can encounter the **living God** and be utterly transformed. The more we engage with this reality, the more we will understand the **very nature of God**—His holiness, His power, and His presence that fills everything.

John, in the Book of Revelation, described the Throne Room in a vision, but this was no mere dream—it was a window into how **things truly are**. The Throne Room is the center of all creation, the place from which the pulse of the universe flows. For those of us who have tasted the power of God, who have seen bodies healed and lives restored, we know that the authority of this Throne Room **breaks into the natural world**. It is not confined to heaven—it touches earth, and when it does, it changes everything.

There are experiences, moments, and realities that we can never fully capture with words or logic. The **Throne Room of God** is one such reality. It is the place where **everything begins and everything returns**, where time, space, and human limitations seem to dissolve in the overwhelming presence of God. The Throne Room is not something we approach with the mind alone—it's a place where **the spirit leads**, and where the deepest parts of our being encounter the **limitless presence of God**.

For those who have experienced even a glimpse of this reality, it changes everything. There is something about the Throne Room that **pulls us beyond** the ordinary, beyond the familiar, and into a realm where God is not only seen or heard but felt. To step into the Throne Room is to step into the **heartbeat of the universe**, where the power of God pulses through everything, where light and life are inseparable, and where **transformation happens instantly**.

Encounters with God are never purely intellectual. They are deeply **experiential**, rooted in the power and presence of God. These encounters are not merely about understanding—they are about **being undone**, being remade, being drawn into a reality that transcends human explanation.

More than just a distant or abstract concept, the Throne Room is a **reality we are invited to enter into** through Christ. The Scriptures reveal that we now have direct access to this throne—not in fear or trepidation but with confidence, because of the work of Jesus. This chapter will explore key passages in the New Testament that describe the Throne Room of God and what it means for believers to approach it boldly, experience its power, and participate in its activity.

A Place of Encounter: The Throne Room as the Seat of Divine Presence

"At once I was in the Spirit, and there before me was a throne in heaven with someone sitting on it."(Revelation 4:2)

One of the most vivid depictions of the **Throne Room of God** comes from the **Book of Revelation**, where the apostle John is given a vision of heaven's glory. In **Revelation 4**, John is caught up in the Spirit and beholds the majesty of God's throne. The scene is one of awe-inspiring beauty and power: a throne surrounded by heavenly beings, with flashes of lightning and peals of thunder. (Revelation 4:5).

John describes the One sitting on the throne as shining like **jasper and carnelian**, and a **rainbow resembling an emerald** encircling the throne. This description points to the **radiant holiness** of God, His purity, and the covenant of mercy that encircles His rule. Around the throne are **twenty-four elders** and **four living creatures**, worshiping day and night, declaring, *"Holy, holy, holy is the Lord God Almighty, who was, and is, and is to come!"* (Revelation 4:8).

When John was lifted into the Spirit and found himself before the **throne**, he didn't just observe—it was as though he was being **drawn into something far deeper** than a vision. The throne is not merely a symbol of authority; it is the **center of all existence**. The throne pulses with the energy of creation, with the full force of God's will, love, and power.

To stand before that throne is not simply to witness God's rule, but to **experience His presence** in a way that transcends anything we can experience on earth. The **lightning and thunder** that surround the throne are not just expressions of power—they are **forces** that radiate the intensity of God's being, as if creation itself is continually responding to the One who sits upon the throne.

When John was caught up in the Spirit and taken into the Throne Room of God, he did not find a place of chaos or uncertainty. He found a **throne**, firmly established, with Someone seated upon it. That vision is a powerful reminder that despite the unpredictability of life, despite the chaos we often see in the world around us, **there is an order, a center, and a sovereign God**.

When we pray, when we believe, when we step out in faith, we are participating in the very energy that flows from God's throne. It's not abstract power; it is living, breathing power—ready to heal, to deliver, and to restore. The throne is not static—it is the source of a divine flow, reaching into the earth and into our very lives.

Kathryn Kuhlman would describe moments when, standing in a meeting, she could sense the air around her **thick with God's presence**. The atmosphere would change, the room would feel alive, and it was as if people were **stepping into that Throne Room reality** right there, in the physical world. Healings would happen spontaneously—not because of her, but because they had **entered into a place** where God's domain was overwhelming. The Throne Room, you see, can invade our space and time in ways we cannot always understand, but we can certainly experience.

"The Throne Room is a place of encounter. It is where God's presence is so thick, so real, that to be near it is to be changed. The power that flows from that throne is not abstract—it's the living presence of God, breaking into our world."

Imagine standing in a room where the very air seems to vibrate with a power that cannot be explained but only felt. This is what the Throne Room is like—not just a vision, but an **encounter with the essence of God**. Everything is alive with His presence, and in that place, no one leaves unchanged.

Prepare for encounter. The Throne Room is not just a place to be observed; it is a place to be experienced. When you draw near to God, expect His presence to manifest in ways that go beyond understanding. It is not just what you will see, but what you will feel—**the weight of His glory**.

God's throne is the center of reality. Everything flows from His authority. The Throne Room reminds us that no matter how chaotic the world seems, God is in control, seated in glory. Worship and confidence in His sovereignty will be our natural response from this place.

Imagine standing in the presence of a throne that radiates light, surrounded by heavenly beings that cry out, *"Holy, holy, holy is the Lord God Almighty."* What John saw was true reality—a God who is not distant, but active, reigning, and manifesting His power in the earth. Every healing is a glimpse of that power, every miracle a whisper of heaven touching earth.

The Throne of Grace: Stepping into a Place Beyond Words

"Let us then approach God's throne of grace
with confidence, so that we may receive mercy and
find grace to help us in our time of need." (Hebrews 4:16)

Now, let's talk about access. This is where many stumble. We read about the glory of God, the majesty of His throne, and we shrink back. How could we, flawed as we are, **approach this throne?** But the author of Hebrews makes something startlingly clear: **we can approach with confidence**. Why? Because it's not about us—it's about **Jesus**. It's His righteousness that has torn down the veil and opened the way for us to enter the Throne Room.

One of the most profound truths the New Testament teaches about the Throne Room is that, through Christ, **we are invited to approach it with confidence**. In the Old Covenant, access to God's throne was limited. The Holy of Holies, where God's presence dwelled, was only accessible to the high priest once a year. But in the New Covenant, the veil has been torn, and believers are given direct access to the very presence of God.

John G. Lake would tell you that the greatest hindrance to seeing God move is not His reluctance but **our unbelief**. When we realize that we have been granted access to the throne of **grace**—where the full weight of God's mercy and power resides—we can pray with the boldness that changes things.

Kathryn Kuhlman often spoke about the deep connection between **surrender and power**. The more we surrender our pride, our fear, and our doubts at the feet of Jesus, the more His grace flows into our lives. The Throne Room, she would say, is not a place to come trembling in fear—it's a place to come with expectation, believing that God is eager to pour out His grace upon His children.

Picture a throne—majestic, glorious, surrounded by angels—and then imagine that God Himself is saying to you, *"Come boldly."* Not in fear, but in **confidence**, knowing that you are loved, accepted, and that His grace is more than enough. This is not a distant hope; it is a present reality for those who are in Christ.

The writer of Hebrews calls this place the **"throne of grace"**—a place where we receive mercy, help, and strength. This throne, once unreachable, is now available to us because of **Jesus' high priestly work**. Hebrews 4:14-16 tells us that since Jesus has ascended into heaven as our great high priest, we can approach God's throne boldly, knowing that we will receive mercy and grace in our times of need.

The Throne Room is not just a distant, heavenly reality—it is the place where we are invited to come as **children of God**, with the full assurance that we are welcome, loved, and accepted. We approach not out of fear but out of confidence, knowing that Jesus has made the way.

Through Christ, the Throne Room is not a place of judgment for us but a place of grace. We come not in our own righteousness but clothed in the righteousness of Jesus, and we are invited to ask for help in our time of need.

As you approach this throne, something beyond words happens. You don't just know about grace—you **feel it**. It surrounds you. It washes over you. It's a tangible experience, where the very essence of God's mercy is something that you don't just believe in, but that you **touch**. This grace becomes a **living force**, working in your life, shaping you, healing you, and drawing you closer to God's heart.

Receive grace beyond understanding. When you approach God's throne, don't just ask—**receive**. Be open to the experience of His presence. This is not a transactional moment; it's an encounter with the living God.

Allow His grace to move beyond your mind and into your heart, where it can heal and restore.

A Place of Transformation: The Throne Room as the Center of God's Holiness

"For we must all appear before the judgment seat of Christ, so that each of us may receive what is due us for the things done while in the body, whether good or bad." (2 Corinthians 5:10)

The New Testament also speaks of the **Throne of God** as a place of judgment. In **2 Corinthians 5:10**, Paul reminds us that we will all stand before the **judgment seat of Christ**. This throne represents the authority of Jesus to evaluate the lives of believers. This is not judgment in terms of condemnation, but it is a moment of **accountability** where our lives, actions, and faithfulness are brought before God.

In Revelation, we also see the **Great White Throne** (Revelation 20:11-12), where all of humanity will stand before God. Books will be opened, including the **Book of Life**, and those whose names are written there will enter eternal life. This throne represents God's ultimate authority to **judge and restore all things**. The Throne Room is not only a place of worship but also where **God's justice** is revealed.

For believers, the Throne Room as a place of judgment is not something to fear. Through Christ, we have been justified, and our sins have been dealt with on the cross. What we will give an account for is how we have lived in light of God's grace and calling. The Throne of God is where His perfect justice meets His perfect mercy, and where all things will ultimately be made right.

The Throne Room is also a place of **judgment**. This is where we must balance our understanding of God. Yes, the throne is a place of grace, but it is also a place of **perfect justice**. God's throne is not only the source of mercy—it is the source of all righteousness. And righteousness demands that every life, every decision, every motive is brought into alignment with **God's holy standard**.

John G. Lake would tell us that this judgment isn't something to fear if we are in Christ—but it is something to take seriously. We must live our lives with the awareness that we will give an account before the **judgment seat of Christ**. But here's the beauty: even God's judgment is redemptive for those who belong to Him. It purifies, restores, and brings us closer to His holiness.

The Throne Room isn't about condemning the believer—it's about **transforming** us. When we encounter the holiness of God, something in us must change. It's impossible to stand in the presence of the Holy One and walk away unchanged. The fire of His holiness burns away the dross and refines us.

Imagine standing before a judge, not one who seeks to condemn, but one who seeks to **restore**. The Throne Room is a place where everything is laid bare, and yet, for those in Christ, it's a place of profound restoration. The justice of God brings healing—it brings clarity, it aligns us with His will.

Live in light of God's holiness. The Throne Room calls us to live lives that reflect God's holy standard. Judgment isn't about fear, but about transformation. Let the reality of God's throne draw you into a deeper walk of purity, integrity, and love.

To step into the Throne Room is to come face-to-face with a **purifying fire** that burns away everything that does not align with His holiness.

When we stand before God's throne, we are not the same afterward. His holiness doesn't just confront us—it changes us. The Throne Room isn't a place to remain comfortable; it's a place where the **deepest parts of us** are exposed, and God's presence burns away what is not of Him.

God's holiness is not to be feared in the way we understand fear—but it is to be **revered**. When we encounter this holiness, something happens in our spirit that words can't fully describe. We are drawn deeper into the **mystery of God's being**, and in that place, we are invited to be changed. You can't stand before His throne and walk away the same. Holiness demands transformation. It's not punitive—it's **restorative**.

Step into God's purifying presence. The Throne Room is a place of transformation. Don't shy away from the holiness of God—allow it to refine you. The fire of His presence is not there to harm you but to cleanse you and draw you deeper into relationship with Him.

Worship and Intercession: Participating in the Unseen Reality

"And they sang a new song, saying: 'You are worthy... because you were slain, and with your blood you purchased for God persons from every tribe and language and people and nation." (Revelation 5:9)

In the New Testament, the Throne Room is portrayed not only as a place of authority and judgment but also as the **center of heavenly worship. In Revelation 5,** John describes a scene where **multitudes of angels,** living creatures, and elders gather around the throne to worship the Lamb. The Lamb, who is Jesus, is declared worthy to receive all glory and honor because He was slain, and by His blood, He redeemed people from every nation and tribe.

This scene in the Throne Room shows that worship in the Throne Room of God is centered on **Jesus Christ, the Lamb who was slain.** All of heaven is captivated by the glory of the Lamb, and they pour out their adoration and praise in response to His sacrifice. In **Revelation 5,** the heavenly beings declare, *"Worthy is the Lamb who was slain, to receive power and wealth and wisdom and strength and honor and glory and praise!"* (Revelation 5:12). This worship is not just an acknowledgment of God's greatness—it is a response to the redemptive work of Christ.

The Lamb who was slain stands at the center of the Throne Room, symbolizing that the cross **and resurrection of Jesus** are at the heart of God's plan for the world. The heavenly worship is a reminder to us that **our lives are also to be centered around Christ**. The Throne Room shows us that worship is not just an earthly act, but a **heavenly reality**—one in which we are invited to participate.

As believers, we are part of the **heavenly chorus**. When we worship here on earth, we are joining the voices of angels, elders, and all creation who worship the Lamb in heaven. Our worship is not isolated or individual—it connects us to the eternal worship that takes place in the very Throne Room of God. This vision calls us to a deeper understanding of what worship truly is: an offering of **honor and praise to Jesus** for who He is and what He has done.

"The Throne Room of God is a place where all creation acknowledges the worth of Jesus Christ, the Lamb who was slain. Worship in the Throne Room is an eternal response to the glory and grace of God revealed through His Son."

Imagine the **angels and saints** surrounding the throne, their voices blending together in perfect harmony as they worship the Lamb. Their worship is a response to Jesus' sacrifice, and they are overwhelmed by the **glory and love** that radiates from Him. Every knee is bowed, every voice is lifted, and the focus is entirely on Christ, the Redeemer.

Worship is at the heart of the Throne Room. Our worship here on earth is a reflection of the worship that takes place in heaven. Let your life be marked by worship, centered on Christ, as you join with all creation in declaring the worth of the Lamb.

Worship in the Throne Room is unlike anything we experience on earth. It's not simply a matter of singing songs or raising hands—it is a **full immersion** into the reality of who God is. In the Throne Room, worship is a **response** to the overwhelming presence of God. It's as though every cell in your body responds to the **worthiness of the Lamb**.

When we worship God in the fullness of who He is, we are not just praising Him for what He's done—we are **joining in the activity of heaven**. Our prayers and our worship are caught up into this divine reality, and they become part of the ongoing **movement of God's will** in the world.

It's in those moments where God's presence is so tangible, so real, that **miracles often happen effortlessly**. The Throne Room is not only a place where God is praised—it is where His power is released into the world. Every prayer offered in this place, every word of worship, carries with it the authority of heaven.

Worship in the Throne Room is a response to the overwhelming presence of God. It is not just something we do—it is something we are caught up into.

Intercession and worship merge in the Throne Room, where heaven's will is enacted on earth.

Imagine standing in a vast expanse of light and sound, where every voice is lifted in perfect harmony, praising the Lamb who was slain. In that place, you don't just hear the worship—you become part of it. Every word, every note is infused with the **power of God's presence**, and it carries with it the authority to change the world.

Engage fully in worship and intercession. When you worship, you are joining in the ongoing activity of heaven. Allow yourself to be **caught up** in the reality of God's throne, where worship and intercession are one and the same. Your prayers and praise carry the authority of heaven.

Living in the Reality of the Throne Room

The Throne Room of God is not simply a distant vision—it is the **center of all things**. Through Christ, we have been given access to this throne, where we find grace, mercy, healing, and the transforming power of God's holiness.

Please recognize that the power of the Throne Room is **available to you now**. In this place, the **miracles of heaven touch earth**. This is not just a theological truth—it is a reality you can live in daily.

The Throne Room is where worship, prayer, judgment, and grace meet, and it is the place where we are called to live our lives—in awe of God's holiness, in confidence of His grace, and in the power of His Spirit.

"The Throne Room of God is the center of all reality. Through Christ, we are invited to enter boldly, receive grace, and be transformed by the power that flows from the very heart of God."

It's where the presence of God is so overwhelming that it changes everything. **John G. Lake** would call you to recognize the tangible power that flows from this place and into our world. **Kathryn Kuhlman** would remind you that it is in the Throne Room where miracles happen, where God's presence is made real in our midst.

This is not just a theological concept; it's a reality we are invited to experience. The Throne Room is where **heaven touches earth**, and it's a place we are called to live from—**in awe, in power, and in love**.

"*The Throne Room is the center of all reality, a place of encounter where God's presence transforms us, His power moves through us, and His holiness purifies us. Step into this place with expectation and allow it to shape your life in ways beyond what you can imagine.*"

ABOUT THE AUTHOR

Philip Brown is a trained leader and educator who is deeply passionate about guiding others into transformative relationships with God. Rooted in Kansas City, he has spent years cultivating a life defined by faith, service, and a heartfelt commitment to seeing the gospel's power at work in real, tangible ways. Whether through teaching, pastoral care, or hands-on outreach, Philip's focus remains on connecting people to God's presence and empowering them to step into their true purpose. His ministry experience spans urban missions, disaster relief efforts, and partnerships with influential leaders. These opportunities have shaped him into a leader who values both the beauty of ancient faith traditions and the relevance of the Spirit's dynamic work in the present.

Having trained at ministry school in Redding, CA, Philip has a background in pastoral care, social justice advocacy, and prayer ministry. His studies under leaders from various denominational streams have informed his holistic approach to ministry—one that integrates scholarship, spiritual gifts, and compassion-driven service. Philip's love for New Testament Scripture, Church History, and relational and interpersonal wellness enriches all he does, making his teaching accessible and inviting to both beginners and seasoned theologians alike. In all his endeavors—preaching, writing, mentoring—Philip Brown remains dedicated to helping others engage with spiritual realities, encounter Christ's transformative love, and carry that love to the world.

www.ingramcontent.com/pod-product-compliance
Lightning Source LLC
Chambersburg PA
CBHW061154120626
46546CB00005B/2057